Beryl Markham

THE BARNARD BIOGRAPHY SERIES

Beryl Markham

Never Turn Back

Catherine Gourley

Foreword by Rosellen Brown

CONARI PRESS
Berkeley, California

Conari Press books are distributed by Publishers Group West

Reprinted by permission of North Point Press, a divison of Farrar, Straus, & Giroux, Inc.: Excerpts from WEST WITH THE NIGHT by Beryl Markham. Copyright © 1942, 1983 by Beryl Markham.

Cover design: Suzanne Albertson
Cover portrait: Lino Saffioti
Photo credit: page xv, UPI/Corbis-Bettmann

ISBN: 1-57324-073-7

Library of Congress Cataloging-in-Publication Data

Gourley, Catherine. 1950–
    Beryl Markham : never turn back / Catherine Gourley : foreword by Rosellen Brown.
        p.   cm. — (The Barnard Biography Series; 1)
    Includes bibliographical references and index.
    Summary: Describes the life of the first person, man or woman, to fly across the Atlantic Ocean from east to west, from her childhood in Africa through many difficulties to her aeronautic and literary achievements.
    ISBN 1-57324-073-7 (trade paper)
    1. Markham Beryl—Juvenile literature.   2. Air pilots—Great Britain—Biography—Juvenile literature.   3. Air Pilots—Africa—Biography—Juvenile literature.   [1. Markham, Beryl.   2. Air pilots.   3. Women—Biography.]   I. Title.   II. Series: Barnard Biography Series (Berkeley, Calif.) ; 1.
TL540.M345G68   1997
629.13' 092—dc20   96–44762
[B]   CIP
                                                AC
Printed in the United States of America on recycled paper
10 9 8 7 6 5 4 3 2 1

For my
sister Maureen

Contents

Foreword

I remember the first time I heard that pearls began as tiny irritations inside oysters—most often, a piece of trapped sand rubbing against tender skin. The oyster's response seemed nothing less than miraculous. Who would believe that the gorgeous translucent shield it created to contain the irritant could become what we call a pearl and value for its beauty?

Whether or not you like pearls or oysters, the process is remarkable, and it turns out to resemble the way our personalities sometimes grow around the painful particulars in our lives, protecting us and making us strong (and sometimes even beautiful) just at the points where we might otherwise fracture or fall apart.

Beryl Markham's life seems to have shaped itself that way, at least in its early years near the beginning of this century. Her father, an ex-Army officer who had a way with horses, decided that his fortune lay in East Africa, where the British (among others) were establishing farms and living contentedly, or so word had it, among lions and leopards and exotic greenery, lush forests, boundless open grazing land. Beryl and her older brother had been born in England; their father must have thought unspoiled Africa would be a healthy, invigorating place to raise his children.

But—the sand in the oyster—there was one complication: his wife Clara, a woman of more conventional tastes, found the rigors of the homestead and the absence of a social life lonely and oppressive. It was difficult to keep her sickly eldest child healthy with the nearest doctor a hundred miles away. When Beryl was four years old, her mother, having sent her son ahead, left husband and daughter and escaped to London and "civilization."

So Beryl found herself alone with her father in the company of the natives of the Kipsigis tribe who worked for him. Abandoned, she hardened herself to the need for a mother and for a mother's affection and instruction, and found her teachers among the people whose land she was borrowing; she gave all her love to her father, to her dogs and horses, and to a warrior named *arap* Maina and his son, Kibii, with whom she roamed the lovely land and learned to swing on vines, run and jump and wrestle, to read the signs the animals left when they passed, to skin a buck, to treat a snake bite. Once she was mauled by a lion, a story she liked to tell (and possibly, when she sat many years later in English and American dining rooms, to embroider).

The "civilization" her mother represented, lace petticoats and high tea, inspired profound contempt in the wild-haired, long-legged child who rode and hunted and learned her way around the stable with the boys and men. Of course it's impossible ever to analyze anyone with perfect confidence, and no one's behavior is simple enough to attribute it to a single cause. Possibly Beryl was born with a high "danger" quotient (since geneticists are beginning to see a need for adventure and physical daring as inborn, like blue eyes or a tendency toward shyness). But who could blame her if her flamboyance and daring were the pearls she made of her defenses? She was physically strong, lovely to look at, capable of hard work and deep concentration. She knew how to learn lessons at the feet of the masters of the bush. And later, when she exchanged her passion for horses for a devotion to a different kind of flight on the steel and canvas horse of her airplane, she was a conscientious student of her flight instructors. She was most comfortable in the kind of pants and loose shirts they wore—the woman she became would not have learned much that was useful from her mother in her silks and her safety. After the death of her dearest teacher, Tom Black, she said, "The knowledge of my hands on the (plane's) controls had been Tom's knowledge." She knew that no one did anything entirely alone.

Beryl craved speed, independence, power; simple feet-on-the-ground contentment she called "a slumber." Given a horse as a young girl, she named him Pegasus for the mythic horse with wings. And whenever anyone tried to put a bridle on her—when she was sent off to a school she had no use for, or dressed in ruffles and made to wear "lady" shoes, or married off at sixteen like the object of a horse trade (some say because her husband had promised, in return for her, to settle her father's considerable debt) —she bucked and threw her rider and galloped off in her own direction.

Eventually, like most uncontrollable forces, she did a lot of damage. Not only did she cast aside two, possibly three, husbands but when Beryl had her own child, a boy named Gervase, incredibly—or predictably?—she did to him exactly what her mother had done to her—without apology, she abandoned him. She left him to be raised entirely by his father.

In 1936, after years of flying (some of it spent on dangerous elephant-spotting missions for hunters), Beryl Markham made herself famous for taking her daring and concentration public. At a time when flying was still primitive and uncomfortable and full of risk, she became the first person, man or woman, to accomplish what was called a "waterjump"—to fly across the Atlantic from east to west, England to Nova Scotia. But for me, because I'm earthbound, in love not with literal flight but with the flight of the mind that takes place in libraries or in my own comfortable chair, Beryl's ultimate achievement was her transformation into a writer. What a remarkable book she made of her life (leaving out, willful as ever, the painful parts). In her memoir, *West with the Night,* she describes not only her vivid childhood but the freedom of the skies, the unrolling of the glorious African land beneath her, as beautifully as anyone has ever done; in part because it was her own experience, not someone else's "as told to" her, and partly because in everything she did (except care for other people) she was hugely talented and fearless.

It does, after all, take fearlessness to be a writer, though surely a different kind than it takes to sit in the cockpit of a tiny plane and listen to your engines struggle and fail. It takes such patience, attentiveness and a passionate desire to communicate experience to those who've never felt it that I doubt anyone who knew her could have predicted that Beryl Markham could turn her physical mastery into something that takes the stillness and silence of good writing. But Beryl was never one to do what others predicted. Out of movement, danger, loss,

loneliness and even anger, she made a lasting and exquis-
ite pearl. Her fellow-writer Ernest Hemingway, whose
much-acclaimed physical courage couldn't begin to rival
hers, said of Beryl, "I knew her fairly well in Africa and
never would have suspected that she could and would put
pen to paper except to write in her flyer's log book. As it
is, she has written so well, and marvelously well, that I
was completely ashamed of myself as a writer."

How mysterious we are in the end, those who dare
and those who don't but who love to borrow their daring,
as close as words can bring us!

Rosellen Brown

A 1960 alumna of Barnard College, Rosellen Brown is the recip-
ient of the Janet Kafka Heidinger Prize in literature. She is the
author of four novels, three collections of poetry, and *The
Rosellen Brown Reader,* a collection of short stories, essays, and
poetry.

Hours after her historic flight across the Atlantic, Beryl told reporters, "When I sighted that swampy field, I thought I could put the plane down all right. Well, I didn't."

In New York, Beryl greets an adoring crowd of well-wishers by raising her arms in a traditional African *salaam*.

one

The Waterjump

Beryl Markham wondered how much longer she could stay awake. Cramped inside the cockpit between two petrol tanks, she had been piloting the single engine airplane for more than nineteen hours without a rest. She had been flying blind, unable to see anything but darkness and fog outside the cabin window. She had been flying silent, without a radio transmitter to guide her or keep her company through the long stormy night. She had been flying without even a life jacket, for there was not enough room inside the cabin to hold that lifesaving equipment and the necessary extra tanks of fuel.

Now at last it was morning and the fog had begun to thin. Through the skin of ice that had formed on the inside of the cabin window, she saw the lights of a ship far below her on the Atlantic Ocean. She felt a sudden exhilaration. Still, she could not be certain just where she was. England and Ireland were behind her. She could only hope that she had not drifted off course and that somewhere ahead, hidden under the ribbons of fog, were the cliffs of Newfoundland.

In September, 1936, no man or woman had ever flown an airplane east to west across the Atlantic Ocean. Beryl was intending to be the first. The airplane that she was piloting was a single engine Vega Gull christened The Messenger. Her friends in England had teased her that it should be called instead The Flying Tombstone. For flying an airplane the wrong way across the Atlantic Ocean was a dangerous thing to attempt. Some had called it suicidal. Strong head winds would slow the plane down and use up most of its fuel. In September, bad weather could skid her off course. Even a few degrees off course could mean not reaching land before her fuel ran out.

"I wouldn't tackle it for a million," J. C. Carberry had told her, even though he was the one who had dared her to do it and then put up the money to build the airplane. "Think of all that black water!" he said, smiling grimly. "Think how cold it is!"

But Beryl had been in dangerous spots before and had used her wits to pull her through. In the highlands of East Africa, where she had spent her childhood, she had been attacked by a lion. She had hunted wild boar with *arap* Maina, a Kipsigis warrior. She had ridden her father's wild stallions across the fields of his farm in Njoro. Beryl Markham rather liked danger. It made her feel alive. She had been afraid to try this incredible waterjump. She had lain in her bed just yesterday morning and considered bailing out of the agreement she had made with J. C. But long ago her father and *arap* Maina had taught her that if a thing were worth doing, then she must swallow her fear and do it well.

At five o'clock the previous afternoon, Beryl had

stood on the airfield in Abingdon, England. The weather forecast was not good: head winds of forty to fifty miles per hour and rolling in off the Atlantic, heavy thunderstorms. A small crowd of newspaper reporters and photographers had gathered at the airfield. They had been dogging her for days. Why are you doing this? they had pressed. Why risk your life?

The names of other pilots—Charles Lindbergh, Amelia Earhart, Jim Mollison—were already in the record books. Like them, Beryl Markham was a professional pilot. She had more than 2,000 hours of flying experience. She cared nothing for setting new records. Nor was she anxious to die. How could she explain to these reporters about her father and *arap* Maina and the lessons they and Africa had taught her? How could they understand why it was important that she swallow her fears and move forward? She couldn't explain it to them. She didn't try. Her answer was simply, "Flying is my job and this Atlantic flight is part of it."

Beryl had crawled into the cockpit and taken off into a rainy sky. Once airborne, confidence and concentration had replaced fear. But now, after nineteen hours of fog and rain and sleet, she was exhausted. The Gull's engine droned. Beryl's eyes burned and her head felt heavy. Her legs and back were cramped. A shadow appeared in the fog ahead. Beryl squinted through the ice on the window, hoping the shadow was land. Then she smiled. Cliffs were standing in the sea, reaching up to her. The land might be Labrador or Newfoundland. Her destination was New York City. But here at least was solid ground. She could follow the coast south to Sydney, Nova Scotia, where she could land, refuel, and take off again. She began to hum. The hard part—the hundreds of miles of cold, black water and the droning loneliness—was nearly over.

Then suddenly, the droning ceased. The engine coughed, then died. The Messenger began to lose altitude. The fuel gauge was near empty, but the plane should still have had enough petrol to make land. A few more miles, Beryl thought as her free hand quickly turned on and off the handles of each empty petrol tank, hoping to unclog what she believed must be an airlock. The handles' sharp metal pins bit into the palms of her hand. The engine caught and climbed, then spat and sputtered and dove again. Beryl stared hard at the cliffs ahead. The boulders on the beach would surely shred the The Messenger's belly. With bleeding hands, Beryl pulled back on the stick to keep the Gull in the air, trying to clear the cliffs. Just a few more miles, she thought, a few more moments.

Again the engine cut out. The single propeller swung slowly, then stopped. The Gull glided, as silent as a sea bird floating above land. The realization that she had failed struck Beryl as hard as the ground rushing up to snag the Gull's nose. The powerful impact threw her forward, smashing her head against the windshield. She heard the glass shatter. Then all was quiet.

two

Lakweit

A voice called to her. *"Lakweit!"* It was the voice of *arap* Maina. "Your eyes are filled with clouds today, *Lakweit!"*

In Swahili, *lakweit* means "little girl." Beryl was no more than seven years old, but already she was tall and slender and strong. Her hair was straw yellow and hung in her eyes. She wore no hair ribbons the way other little British girls living in East Africa in 1909 did. Instead, a cowrie shell hung around her waist on a leather cord. The Africans who worked for Charles Clutterbuck, Beryl's father, had tied the shell around her in order to keep away evil spirits.

"Lakweit! Bend down and look so that you may learn." *Arap* Maina was the African whom Beryl's father had assigned as the child's personal servant. *Arap* was a term of respect, and Beryl listened carefully to her guardian. "See how this leaf is crushed. Feel the wetness of this dung."

He was her teacher, and her classroom was the Great Rift Valley in the country that would become known,

5

years later, as Kenya. At the beginning of the twentieth century, British pioneers like Charles Clutterbuck controlled the land. Beryl was the daughter of *mazungu,* the white man. She had a mother, but Clara Clutterbuck had gone away long ago. The Kipsigis and Nandi peoples, Africans from two different tribes who worked for Clutterbuck on his farm in Njoro, had accepted his *lakweit* into their lives without question.

Very often Beryl woke before dawn and stood barefoot in grass as high as her shoulders and still wet and cold with night dew. Before her, the valley turned purple in the morning sunlight. Behind her were the stables that housed her father's racehorses and, beyond the stables, the tall blue cedars of the Mau Forest. Very soon, the *syces,* or African servants, would begin shoveling the manure out of the horse stalls and into the spreading sunshine. But by then, Beryl and her dog, Buller, would be gone, having silently escaped across the valley to be with *arap* Maina and Kibii.

Kibii was *arap* Maina's son. He was younger than Beryl by a few years, but the two children—one female and British, the other male and African—spent their days together. Swinging on vines, wrestling with each other, jumping straight up as high as they could, hiding in wild pig holes—games like these were more than just play. They were an important part of an African child's education. Like Kibii and the other *totos,* or children, Beryl played hard. The games shaped her young muscles and sharpened her senses. She learned how to read a crushed leaf and wet dung and know what wild creature—a water buffalo or a zebra—had passed. Beryl had not yet been to a formal school, but she knew many things. She knew how to skin a buck, how to catch moles for the money her father paid her, how to treat a snakebite. And although she had not yet shot a gun or thrown a spear, she knew that the best way to lame a charging lion was to wound him in the shoulder.

Each morning the head *syce* rang the large bell near the stables to announce the beginning of another day of work. Before anyone could stop her, Beryl would begin to run, a sort of hop and skip gait that she had learned by imitating the Nandi warriors. The ground over which she loped had been formed by volcanic eruptions more than 15 million years ago when one continent—Africa—had collided with another—Eurasia. In the violence of that collision, the walls of the Great Rift rose thousands of feet above sea level, cradling an immense valley.

Volcanic eruptions had shaped the land, giving it unique characteristics—sheer, jagged cliffs, a flat floor of desert bush with scattered thorn trees. Now the land was shaping Beryl. Its spine of volcanic rubble still poked through the spongy valley floor, but Beryl's bare feet had long ago toughened to its sharpness. At seven years old, she was already a lover of all things wild and free. The highlands was her home, and her home was alive with the chatter and rumble of a thousand living things. Her home was the whistle and click of reedbuck darting through the grass. It was the bark of leopards stalking close to the white settlers' houses, hunting their domesticated dogs. It was the scratch-scratch of dik-diks no bigger than rabbits using their hind legs to cover their droppings. The voice of *arap* Maina called to her. The voice of

7

the land called to her, too. And *Lakweit* ran, answering the call.

But life for Beryl would not remain so wild and free for very long. Many pioneer settlers in the highlands did not approve of the way Charles Clutterbuck—called Clutt by his friends—was raising his daughter. It was not proper for a white child, a girl particularly, to run wild like some creature in the bush, sniffing animal dung. Why was she not at home learning arithmetic and British history? Nor was it proper for her to roam unchaperoned among the Africans whose morals were clearly not the same as theirs. The cowrie shell was an example. Was it not the symbol of female genitalia? The Kipsigis tied the shell around the waists of their own female children soon after birth. Yes, something had to be done about Clutt's wild child. After all, Beryl was a British subject.

Beryl Clutterbuck was born in England on October 26, 1902. She was the second child. Her brother Richard was two years older. Her Irish mother, Clara Alexander, was an excellent horsewoman. Clara's greatest love was fox hunting, a sport that was challenging to even the best equestrian. Soon after Beryl was born, Clara was thundering again through fields and woods on her horse, chasing fox.

Clutt was also a strong rider. He had once been an officer in the army, but by the time Beryl was born, his occupation was listed on the child's birth certificate as farmer. What Clutt knew best was how to handle horses. In 1904, he began to consider leaving England and its ruddy fox for a wilder place with fiercer game—the high-lands of East Africa. The British government had recently gained control of that part of Africa. It called its newest colony BEA, for British East Africa, and described its occu-pation as a protectorate, a superior power in control over a dependent people. Now it was offering parcels of African land to British citizens for the low price of approx-imately seven cents an acre. Here was a country where every white settler could be the lord of his own manor. The red soil was so rich that sweet potatoes could grow to forty pounds, or so the rumors went. To encourage white settlement, the government had just completed the con-struction of a railroad line from the harbor town of Mombasa on the Indian Ocean inland to Nairobi. From there, the train line struggled upcountry nine thousand feet into the highlands and across the Great Rift Valley, ending at Kisumu on Lake Victoria.

The Africans called the line the Iron Snake. In England, they called it the Lunatic Line, a train to nowhere. Many people believed that the altitude of the mountains was too high for the air to be healthy and that the equatorial sun could weaken the heart, liver, and spleen of light-skinned Europeans. The "town" of Nairobi was nothing more than a cluster of tin shacks along the rail line. Beyond Nairobi, the country had no roads, no hospitals, and few farms.

Then there was the resistance of the Africans. The Kikuyu, in particular, viewed the white settlers as invaders and used poison-tipped arrows to drive them off their land. To maintain control and to display superior force, a small British army known as the Third Battalion of the

King's African Rifles (KAR) patrolled the colony, putting down with bullet and bayonet what the British referred to as "savage" rebellions.

If Clutt knew about the poison-tipped arrows of the Kikuyus or the bayonets of the KAR, it did not change his mind. Six weeks after learning about the land for sale in BEA, Clutt sold most everything that he and Clara owned. Beryl was not even two years old and her brother just four when the family left England, taking with them some pieces of antique furniture and an English sheepdog. Beryl remembered only sailing for a long time on a ship that seemed to climb "the hill of the sea and never reach[ed] the top."

In the highlands, days are hot and sunny and dry. The nights are often cold enough for frost. Charles found work managing a dairy owned by a British aristocrat who had also emigrated to BEA, Lord Hugh Cholmondeley Delamere. Lord Delamere called his African home on the foothills of the Mau Forest "Equator Ranch," because the equator ran through one corner of his property. Even so, Delamere hated the sun. He had once become very ill with sun sickness, and every day as he rode across his thousands of acres, inspecting barbed wire fences and the health of his cattle, he wore a large pith helmet to shade his face. His red hair hung long to his shoulders and protected his neck from the sun. Lord Delamere was not the only one who feared the sun. A common article of clothing worn by the settlers was a spine pad, a sort of flannel belt or cummerbund that Europeans believed could prevent the rays of the sun from damaging vital internal organs.

Lord Delamere and his wife Florence became two of the most influential of the white settlers in BEA. Although they were lord and lady, the Delameres lived as most settlers did in a mud hut called a *rondavel*. The dark walls of mud were cool against the beating sun. At night when temperatures dropped low enough for frost, the mud walls prevented drafts. The floor of the hut was also made of earth, tamped and polished as smooth as clay, but unlevel just the same. The Delameres' wooden dining table and sideboard sat at cockeyed angles inside the hut.

Glass windows and wooden doors with locks might have been practical in England, but not in BEA. A burlap sack worked just as well. The Delameres' front door faced the sweeping plains below, thick with herds of zebra and wildebeest and Thompson's gazelles—called Tommies by the British—that had roamed there long before the Iron Snake found its way into the highlands.

Clara and her children lived in a similar hut on the Delameres' land while Clutt managed the dairy. For Clara, living inside a mud shanty and eating tinned peaches and fresh-butchered Tommy chops for breakfast, lunch, and often again for dinner was a primitive way of life, even if the cooked chops were served on china dishes shipped from England. But at least Clara and her children had a friend in Florence. Like Clara, Florence was Irish. Once, she had also enjoyed foxhunting and dancing and dresses of chiffon and lace. But this was a different place and a different time. The men rose at four in the morning. As the dawn broke, Clara might have heard Delamere's gramophone playing one of his favorite melodies. As the day ended, she might have heard the clamor of voices from the Masai herdsmen who crowded with their spears inside the Delameres' hut to talk of cattle and to share their own folktales. Between sunrise and sunset, the women pioneers worked as hard as the men. They hunted game. They butchered their own meat. They cared for the livestock, including chickens, pigs, and ostriches.

With Delamere's help, Clutt was able to stake his own farm at Njoro. He called it Green Hill Farm. Nothing could be planted in the red soil, however, until the snarls of grass, boulders, and ant hills were cleared away. Years later in her autobiographical book, *West with the Night,* Beryl described the farm at Njoro:

"It looked like this at first: It was a broad stretch of land, part of it open valley, but most of it roofed with the heads of high trees—cedar, ebony, mahogo, teak, and bamboo—and their trunks were snared in miles of creeping plants. The creeping plants rose to heights of twelve and fifteen feet and, from the ground, you never saw the tops of the trees until they fell from the blows of axes and were dragged away by teams of oxen handled by Dutchmen with whips that cracked all day."

Clara did not last long in this wild land so high in the mountains above the sea. She was unhappy. Perhaps it was the elevation. It took time for the body to adjust to the thin, sparkling air at eight thousand feet. Perhaps it was wildlife—the smell of lion on the hot wind—or the insects that bored into the cool mud walls of her rondavel. Lizards clung with webbed feet from the thatch ceiling. Jiggas, a small burrowing insect, lived in the dirt floors. If not careful, a person might discover that the jig-gas had burrowed under her toenails and laid a sack of eggs. Or it might have been the ants. Outside, red anthills as solid as rock spiraled as high as four and five feet or higher. Inside, the legs of the tables, chairs, and beds sat in pans of kerosene that soaked into the wood and kept the ants down.

Or perhaps Clara was simply bored with Clutt and lonely for that other place and time, the soft green of England and a cottage with a real door and glass windows. Lady Delamere might have been contented to sleep with a revolver under her pillow, but Clara had had enough. Richard had a hard time of it, too. Beryl's brother was often ill, and the only doctor was a hundred miles away. And so, in 1906, after two years as a pioneer, Clara arranged for Richard to travel with friends by ship back to England. A few weeks later, she left her husband and Green Hill Farm and followed Richard home to England. Also left behind in the highlands were her English sheepdog and four-year-old Beryl.

Family is very important in almost every African tribe. An African mother would never abandon a healthy child. And so *arap* Maina and his people, the Kipsigis, welcomed Beryl as one of their own. They tied the cowrie shell about her waist to protect her from all the evil in the world. She learned to wrestle and to jump almost as high as her head. She learned how to run silently—skip-hop style—through the grass. She became *Lakweit*. As weeks and then months passed, she forgot what her mother looked like. In time, she forgot all about her. She still had her father, whom the Africans called Cluttabucki. She had her father's horses. She had Buller, an offspring of Clara's sheepdog and one of Lord

13

Delamere's bull terriers. But most important, she had *arap* Maina and Kibii.

But she should wear shoes, the other white settlers argued, and a dress and a hat to protect herself from the sun in the afternoons. She should learn to read and to write, they told Clutt, not how to throw a spear. At other farms, European girls napped in the hot afternoons. They learned how to speak respectfully to their elders and to serve tea. Many settlers felt Clutt was simply a bad father.

But not Beryl. To her, Clutt was powerful. He was not a very tall man, just 5'7", but he could do anything. "The farm at Njoro was endless," she would write years later, remembering her childhood. "But it was no farm at all until my father made it. He made it out of nothing and out of everything—the things of which all farms are made. He made it out of forest and bush, rocks, new earth, sun, and torrents of warm rain. He made it out of labour and out of patience."

Clutt established the first important mill in BEA. The wood from the cedar trees his workers felled in the Mau Forest fed the engines of the Iron Snake. To a seven-year-old, Clutt must have seemed a giant. He made the trains run.

Beryl wanted to please him and to be like him— strong and independent. "People go around kissing and fussing over their children," Beryl once told a newspaper reporter. "I didn't get anything like that. I had to look after myself. . . ." She also wanted to be like *arap* Maina— clever and brave. What she did not want was to wear shoes and a dress and study arithmetic. In England, shoes might be as practical as doors and windows. But in Africa, bare feet worked just as well.

But even Clutt realized that his little girl needed someone in the home to care for her. He had a farm to chisel out of the thick cedars and mahogos in the Mau Forest. He had racehorses to train and sell. What he did not have was time to babysit or coddle a little girl. It was unlikely that Clara would ever return to Africa. Clutt himself had grown up motherless. His mother, Mary Rose Clutterbuck, had died when Clutt was just three months old. A nanny had cared for him for eight years until his father remarried.

The disdain of the white neighbors toward him as a father, the mother who was not returning to Africa, the memory of the nanny who had looked after him as a child—one or all of these things could have spurred Clutt's decision to hire Ada Orchardson as a housekeeper.

Ada was young and attractive. She was married and had a son, Arthur, who was the same age as Beryl. Ada's husband was an anthropologist who was studying the Kipsigis people and living among them in their villages. He rarely returned to Nairobi to visit his wife and son. To Clutt, Ada must have seemed the perfect solution to his problems. The housekeeper could chaperone Beryl and teach her school subjects. Perhaps in time, she might even replace the affections of the mother Beryl had lost. Likewise, Arthur could be Beryl's playmate and perhaps, in time, replace the friendship of the brother who had also been lost. And so, Ada and Arthur moved to Green Hill Farm.

This is what Ada found: a wild, little girl who spoke Swahili instead of English, who ran about half naked and ate with her bare hands the way the Africans did, who slept with beads strung along her bed to chase away the devil, who slipped spiders and snakes into Ada's bed, perhaps to chase her away, too. The housekeeper's job was to control Beryl, to civilize her the way Clutt and the other European settlers were civilizing the land. Ada must have sighed a deep, heavy sigh when she first confronted Beryl. How was she to teach this child manners and respect? Her task was not going to be easy.

This is what Beryl saw: a woman with dark hair and violet eyes and smooth, clear skin; a woman whom Arthur called "Mum." But Beryl saw and heard something more, for *arap* Maina had trained *Lakweit* to look closely at things and to learn. Beryl noticed that the other European women whispered about Mum or stopped talking altogether whenever Beryl or Arthur showed up. Beryl saw, too, that Clutt liked Ada. He seemed to like her, in fact, very much. One day, Clutt took Ada's side when she demanded that Beryl put on her shoes. For the first time, Beryl felt something new inside herself unlike any other thing she had felt before—jealousy.

Beryl ran away, every chance she could, not wanting to be in the same house as Mum. Barefoot, she and Buller disappeared through the tunnel of wet grass. She never tired of running. She was *Lakweit*, and *arap* Maina was calling her, and all the living things that were Africa were calling her. Mum could not make her do anything she did not want to do. *Lakweit* would resist. She would find a way.

three

The Escape

I n 1909, the year Ada Orchardson arrived at Green Hill
Farm, the white settlement in the East Africa highlands
was growing rapidly. The Iron Snake carried much more
than pioneers inland and upcountry. The train carried
rams and cattle imported from England for crossbreeding
with local animals. It carried racehorses imported from
many different countries. Tin bathtubs, equipment to run
machines to process coffee beans, burlap sacks of seed for
planting, wooden spools of barbed wire for fences—all the
stuff of civilization arrived by train. Nairobi grew from a
cluster of tin-roofed shacks to a city with hotels and busi-
nesses and muddy streets.

As the train pulled away from the station in Nairobi,
the gusts of steam from the engine sounded like the
grunts of a large animal. The engine picked up steam,
spewing dust and wood sparks as it began its long climb
into the highlands. The cars shimmied over the sun-hot
rails. Inside, passengers sipped tepid drinks and played
cards to pass the drowsy, swaying time. Beyond the red
dust that coated the windows, the land on either side of

17

the track stretched to the horizon, populated with herds of giraffe and gazelles.

"Until you actually saw it and travelled across it . . ." wrote Elspeth Huxley who, like Beryl, was a child when she first came to the highlands in 1913, "you could not possibly grasp the enormous vastness of Africa . . . beyond each range of hills lay another far horizon; always it was the same, pale-brown grass and bush and thorn-trees, rocky mountains, dark valleys, sunlit plains. . ."

Green Hill Farm had also grown. On his 1,500 acres, Clutt now grew maize and wheat. Before harvest, the stalks of maize were taller than a grown man. The farm was more like a factory now. The millstone turned continuously, grinding corn and wheat into meal. The timber mill processed more fuel for the trains. Huge piles of sawdust smoldered day and night near the track, smelling of cedar. But such progress had come with a price. The tribal ways of life had been shattered by force and for profit. More than 1,000 Africans worked for Clutt, but not because they were hungry for work or wages. They labored, in part, to satisfy a hut tax imposed upon them by the government of the protectorate.

The British money system was of little value to the Africans. Sheep and cattle, not coins, were wealth to them. Still, on payday, the Africans stood in a long line, and Beryl watched as her father counted out each wage. As a child, she could not have understood what a feudal system was or that peasants toiled for a lord in exchange for the right to live on his land. She might not have known that some Africans simply buried the coins they were paid. What she knew was that her father was a powerful person. He was *mazungu,* the white man. He had beaten back the mighty Mau Forest to build a farm at Njoro.

With prosperity came a proper house built of wood with glass windows, separate rooms, a large stone fireplace, and a door that closed. In this new house, Africans also worked. Each man wore a *kanzu,* or white robe, that indicated his role as a servant. At night, Clutt sat at his desk with a pint of beer beside him and studied his accounting books. One book, in particular, held great interest for Beryl. It was bound in black leather and thick with pages of notes that Clutt had recorded about his thoroughbreds, for the stables, like everything else, had grown. The black book was important by Beryl's estimation, simply because her father gave it so much of his attention.

As a curious child—and Beryl was always curious—she must have stolen the great book once or twice to try and unlock its mysteries. She later remembered that the handwriting on its pages was "bold and important."

The thoroughbreds in Clutt's stables were an important link between Beryl and Clutt. They brought father and daughter together without the presence of the dreaded Ada Orchardson. Mum never walked through the stables, calming the horses by running a confident hand over their quivering necks. Nor did she ride alongside Clutt in the early morning for a special visit to the Delameres' ranch. But these things—and more—Beryl did.

She had inherited her father's—and perhaps even her mother's—knowledge and sensitivity to the needs of high-strung horses. To snatch more of her father's time and attention, Beryl made herself as useful to him in the stables as she could. She groomed the animals, currying their glossy flanks and digging the red highland mud from their hooves. She went with her father to the races in Nairobi, riding in the train's stable car to keep the horses calm during the rocking one-hundred-mile journey.

These private trips to the Nairobi racetrack and shared rides through the highlands were special moments for Beryl. Clutt had not much liked school. But he had excelled at mythology, and he told her stories of the Greek gods and goddesses. Diana was the powerful hunter. Pegasus was a horse with wings. But in 1909, horse races were held only twice a year. And social visits to the Delameres or the Elkingtons were not so frequent. During the day, Clutt was too busy running his farm, his mill, and his stables to tell Beryl stories. And in the evening there were those books to ponder and scribble into, especially that black leather book.

There was also Ada.

Perhaps Beryl was eight years old when Ada first came to Green Hill Farms. Or maybe she was still seven. It is hard to know for certain for Beryl did not celebrate birthdays. Mary Lovell, one of Beryl's biographers, wrote that Clutt might have aged his daughter the same way he aged the glossy thoroughbreds in his stables. In BEA, the birth dates of all horses was the same—August 1. Clutt could never quite remember Beryl's birthday or her age.

Beryl herself marked her own age by memories of horses. "Horses . . . have been as much a part of my life as past birthdays," she wrote. "I remember them more clearly. There is no phase of my childhood I cannot recall by remembering a horse I owned then or one my father owned or one I knew."

The part of her childhood she did not wish to talk or write about was Ada. Ada was living in the house, of course. But Beryl was not. Beryl's relationship with Arthur was friendly, but her spiteful pranks against the woman who was becoming much more than a housekeeper to Clutt had resulted in Beryl's living in her own rondavel with Buller. No doubt, Beryl considered her faithful dog and the lizards that clung with webbed feet to the mud walls better company than Mum. Immediately after dinner and sometimes even during the meal, Beryl made excuses to escape the large house and Ada's presence. She pretended to return to her hut, but many nights she escaped to be with Kibii. While Clutt and Ada, and perhaps even Arthur, sat quietly in front of the smoking cedar fire in the living room, *Lakweit* huddled near a village fire and listened to the stories the Kipsigis told. Their stories, like Clutt's, were also of gods and witches and magic.

Ada might have discovered Beryl's night escapes. Or maybe she had simply had enough of the spiders in her bed. Mum simply could not control Beryl, let alone educate her. And so Miss Le May arrived at Green Hill Farm. It is not clear who summoned her—Ada or Clutt. However it happened Miss Le May did not replace Ada. Nor did she have intention of replacing the lost affections of the mother who had abandoned Beryl. She was strictly a schoolmarm, practical and severe in her discipline.

Lessons were held in the big house. On the dining

room table lay *The Fundamentals of English Grammar* and *Exercises in Practical Arithmetic.* On the table also was a black ruler. Miss Le May's teaching plan was not complicated. Either you studied and made the right response or you got a sharp crack of the ruler across your knuckles. That was that.

Beryl had long been playing *bao,* a counting game the African *totos* had taught her. She knew her numbers. She just didn't want to spend her time adding and subtracting columns of numbers. Courage and self-control kept Beryl from crying out when Miss Le May's sharp-edged ruler bit her fingers. *Arap* Maina and Kibii had taught *Lakweit* such self-control. Though Kibii might have respected Beryl's endurance of pain, Miss Le May found it infuriating. It was just another example of the girl's boldness and defiance. Soon, the schoolmarm gave up the ruler and armed herself instead with a rhino-hide whip.

No doubt, Miss Le May wore the proper clothes for a woman of her era and position: a long skirt, a blouse with a high, tight collar and long sleeves despite the highlands' noontime heat. Perhaps she even wore a flannel spine pad. Nearby was her *double terai,* a heavy felt hat worn by white women in East Africa, but never worn by Beryl. The girl, in contrast, wore khaki pants and a loose-fitting white shirt and was, as usual, barefoot. Silent and stubborn, she stared back at her governess. The snap of the rhino-hide whip split the air. But *Lakweit* did not flinch.

Arthur was not so arrogant. He studied his grammar and added, subtracted, and multiplied without error and so escaped being whipped. Beryl never faulted him for this. He could do as he wished. But for herself, she would resist. Her father had not "let education get the better of him," and she would not either. She never told Clutt about the whippings for that would be admitting a weakness, and in Africa, Beryl knew, the weak do not survive. Arthur must have witnessed the whippings, which often resulted in broken skin and bleeding. But apparently he never spoke of them, either. Nor would Beryl have wanted him to tell on her behalf. Depending on others to do what you would not was just another weakness. And so the whippings continued, until one day.

A hard rain was falling. Both Clutt and Ada were away from the farm and not expected back for at least one more day. In her father's absence, Beryl's behavior might have been even bolder, more rebellious than usual. What crime she had committed, Beryl never revealed. But the punishment she remembered well. Miss Le May locked her in a dark hut with the windows shuttered tight.

Another girl might have shouted and pounded on the shutters. But Beryl was more clever than that. She knew tantrums could not solve her problem. Stealth was a better strategy. About nine o'clock at night, she made good her escape by using an ivory elephant tusk to "hammer down the window." Once more into the night, Beryl escaped.

It was not the first time she had run away from Miss Le May or from Ada. Sometimes she hid in the stalls of one of her father's stallions. The horse's stamping hooves and bared teeth prevented Miss Le May from entering and dragging her out. Sometimes Beryl fled to be with Kibii and *arap* Maina. This time, for whatever reason, perhaps because of the heavy rain, she hid in a wild pig hole. It was a large enough opening, more like a cave in the side of a hill. The warthogs backed themselves into it, hindquarters first, so as to face any enemy that may be lurking outside when they emerged again.

Into this hole with its loose dirt and dust Beryl crawled, and then she waited. But for what did she wait? For her father to return from the Mau Forest where he had gone to supervise the cutting of new timber? That could be a long time. For the rains to stop? That could be days as well.

Who knows what thoughts worried her throughout that night and into the morning. She was wet and wearing only cotton pajamas. Even snug inside the pig hole, the night would have been chillingly cold so high in the mountains. She was just a child and things frightened her. All around her, she would have heard the grunts and barks of the night hunters—including the leopards that came down from the trees to stalk the dogs of the white settlers.

But the thing that frightened her more than anything else made no sound at all—Siafu.

Siafu are ants, but not just any kind of ants. They are soldier ants with red, armor-like bodies and pincer-jaws that do not sting, but take chunks of flesh from their victims. They move in the millions, in a column like soldiers. Their nests are in the ground, usually near water. But Beryl had heard stories from the Africans that when the rains came, Siafu moved from their nests to higher ground. Siafu attack the soft parts of an animal, the eyes and the nose. Perhaps Beryl had also heard the same story C. W. Kobley had heard and written about in his book

Kenya. "Native hunters say that this ant is the thing an elephant is really afraid of . . . ," he wrote, "they'll enter the trunk and the story goes the elephants go mad with pain and beat their heads against a tree until death."

Beryl knew of, and perhaps had even witnessed, Siafu attacking a horse in its stall. In *West with the Night,* she wrote: "Within a few hours a normal, healthy horse, if he is unable to escape his stable, can be killed and half-eaten by even a reserve division of siafu."

"I have dreamed about a lot of unpleasant things," she wrote, ". . . snakes, drowning, leopard, falling off high places; but the dreams I have had about Siafu, in my bed, under the floor, in my hair . . ." Siafu, in short, were Beryl's worst nightmare.

Somehow she survived the cold night and the rain. The Siafu, if they were on the march, had not found her. She had swallowed her fears. But now she was hungry, and so she crawled out of the pig hole and began to hunt for something to eat.

Clearly, Miss Le May must have been angry to discover that Beryl had escaped her punishment. But the governess's anger must have grown into real alarm when the child did not return. The pounding rain continued. For four days, rain fell and fell, and still Beryl was missing.

"Miss Le May sent staff out to look for Beryl," wrote Errol Trzebinski, one of Beryl's biographers, "but she was nowhere to be found."

By then, Clutt and Ada returned. "Clutterbuck was understandably frantic with worry," wrote Trzebinski. He saddled a horse and rode at once to search for her himself.

In the morning, he returned to the farm alone. He changed horses and started out again.

Ten miles from the farm, he spied her at last. She was running—*Lakweit* was always running—through the long grass. He spurred his horse after her and caught her. She told him she had spent one night with an African tribe, and they had promised not to tell anyone where she was. What she did not tell her father was why she had run away.

Apparently, Clutt excused her behavior as another of his daughter's wild antics that no one, except for possibly himself and *arap* Maina, seemed able to control. The daily lessons resumed. Miss Le May stood over her two pupils at the dining room table. Once again she held in her hand the black ruler. And once again, she rapped the bold girl's knuckles for each wrong answer.

After a few weeks, Beryl decided the game must stop. Clutt was somewhere nearby and that very well might have been why Beryl reacted the way she did. "My hands were so sore that I could barely hold a pencil," Trzybinski reported Beryl as saying. When the ruler came down again, Beryl "yelped loudly, purposely to attract his attention. . . . The howl had the desired effect as my father came rushing in to see what had happened. When he saw the condition of my hands . . . he was so angry that he dismissed the governess there and then."

Or so Beryl said.

Just as it was hard to know for certain how old she was when Ada and Miss Le May entered her life, it was also hard to know for certain when Beryl was telling the truth. She enjoyed listening to the myths her father

26

sometimes told her just as she enjoyed the folktales and legends of witchcraft and magic the Africans told. Possibly she exaggerated the story of Miss Le May, changing it so that her father came to her rescue. She so often wanted her father's attention and so infrequently got it that the story would have pleased her.

No matter how it occurred, Miss Le May left Green Hill Farm. Ada, however, was not about to go away.

four

Night of Lions,
Night of Leopards

Leopards had killed Storm and Sleet, Clutt's grey-hounds, during the night. It often happened in the dark—the killing of a domesticated animal by a more wild, more hungry, and therefore, more determined animal of the bush. Beryl called these dark times nights of lions, nights of leopards.

Despite the fences the white settlers had erected, the land had not been tamed. Lions were still a threat to horses and to humans, and at night cattle were rounded into iron pens called *bomas*. Beryl remembered one such night when a lion had stalked the cattle inside the paddock on Green Hill Farm. The first alert was the bawling of a steer. The *syces* stirred into wakefulness. In the big house, Clutt had heard the disturbance too and reached for a burning hurricane lamp and his rifle. Beryl slipped from her bed and followed the sounds of disturbance outside. In the darkness she spied the shape of a yellow-brown cat dragging through the high grass its kill, a young bull. One moment, the men and their guns were silent; the next moment, a barrage of bullets exploded into the cold night. The lion fled, the dead bullock still in its powerful jaws. Beryl watched "the lion leaping, bullock and all, over the cedar fence." The shooting stopped, and the men lowered their rifles. The lion had escaped.

Other nights were leopard nights. Beryl remembered them as moonlit. The cats slunk close to the house. Their prey were not the cattle in the paddocks but the dogs asleep on the porches. After losing Storm and Sleet, Clutt took matters into his own hands. Tracking the leopard was not practical. The animal's spoor was hard to follow through the bush. Besides, there were many leopards, and he had other tasks in managing the farm that required his time and energy during the daylight. No, it was best to lure the leopard back again at night with bait. Some settlers believed the best way to bait a leopard was to use a chunk of stinking meat in a steel trap that would snap on the leopard's leg. The only way the creature could escape the steel jaws was to chew off its own foot.

Clutt chose a different way.

He tied a young goat to a tree and waited, Beryl beside him in the moonlight. "My father and I crouched by the bulk of a Dutchman's wagon on the edge of the water tank," she wrote. She heard "the smooth snick of cartridges" as her father loaded his rifle. And still they waited. She was afraid, though not for herself. She fixed her eyes on the nervous goat. The animal's instincts told it that being alone in the moonlight in the bush was wrong. It pulled but it could not free itself from the rope that held it to the tree.

And then the shadow of the leopard appeared. Beryl's

muscles tightened. Beside her, her father slowly lifted his rifle to take aim. Beryl remembered "the gliding prowler sleek as a shadow on still water; eyes along the black barrels, the pressure of a finger."

"I always felt . . . so sorry for the little goat," Beryl said, "as I watched it cower with fear as the leopard approached and shuddered to think what would happen to the poor thing, should my father fire too late . . . or his aim be poor."

But Clutt never missed. Some nights, Beryl recalled, her father shot two or even three leopards.

The lesson of the leopard and the goat was one that Beryl's father taught her well. She never forgot it. The lesson was this: She lived in a world of absolutes. You were either victor or victim. In Africa, there was no middle ground, no halfway point, no compromise. Either you shot the leopard or you missed. If you shot the leopard, you saved the goat. If you missed, the goat died. There were no second chances at life.

One night, a leopard took Buller.

Buller was not a lap dog. He weighed almost sixty-five pounds. He was not very pretty to look at, either, a mix between Clara's English sheepdog and one of Lord Delamere's bull terriers. In fact, Beryl thought him ugly. His head and legs were battle-scarred with encounters with cats and wart hogs. But that made him all the more impressive to her. Buller was Beryl's loyal companion, a survivor in her African world of absolutes. He followed her everywhere. Loyalty was respected in Beryl's world. It required action, aggressiveness. Sentimentality, on the other hand, she did not respect. That required only fawning and affection. Neither *arap* Maina nor her father made public displays of affection. So it was with Buller. He was not a dog to be cuddled or petted or to give wet, sentimental kisses. That would have been beneath him, a weakness.

Because he was loyal, he slept at the foot of Beryl's bed in her private rondavel away from Clutt and Ada. On this particular leopard night, the sky was overcast and dark. A furious roar and scream woke Beryl. The leopard had surprised her and Buller both. "Before I could do much more than scramble out of bed," Beryl wrote in *West with the Night,* "dog and leopard disappeared in the moonless night."

Clutt must have heard the furious attack, too. Once more he reached for his hurricane lamp and his rifle. This time, he pursued the leopard, with Beryl following him, into the bush. The trail of blood was fresh under the lamp's glow. But the hunt was in vain. The trail seemed to disappear without a trace of the leopard or Buller. Clutt turned back and took Beryl with him.

Either you were loyal or you were sentimental. Buller had been loyal to Beryl. Now it was time for *Lakweit* to return the faithfulness. At dawn, before the head *syce* had rung the bell to start the work day, she slipped out of her *rondavel* and resumed the hunt. "I set out again and found Buller, barely breathing, his hard skull and his lower jaw pierced as if they had been skewered. I ran for help and carried him back on a stretcher made of sacking. He recovered, after ten months' tedious nursing, and became the same Buller again . . ."

"As for the leopard," Beryl continued, "we caught him

the next night in a trap, but he was beyond all caring anyway. He had no ears, only part of a throat, and great disillusionment in his handsome eyes. To my knowledge, and I think to his, it was the first time any dog of any size had been caught by a leopard and lived to dream about it."

Beryl lived in a world of absolutes. Either you were male or female, black or white, a leopard or a goat. In this world of absolutes, the lion was a predator. There was no in-between for the lion. It could not be a pet. But there was such an animal, and its name was Paddy.

The lion belonged to Jim Elkington, a friend of Clutt's when they had both lived in England. Elkington, in fact, had been one of the people who had sparked Clutt's interest in emigrating to East Africa. Now settled on that other continent, they were neighbors again. Elkington had a ranch near Nairobi. He also had a pet lion that he had rescued from certain death as a cub when its mother had been shot by accident. In Clutt's mind, that was Elkington's first bad judgment. In the wild, some orphaned animals died in order that other animals should live. Elkington's second bad judgment was allowing the fully grown Paddy with his black mane to roam freely on the ranch.

Clutt warned Beryl about Paddy one day while they rode together—she on Wee MacGregor, the stallion pony her father had bought for her—to the Elkington ranch for a visit. The journey was one of the rare moments when Beryl had her father to herself. Instead of telling her stories about the gods on Mount Olympus, however, this time he told her about the courage of lions.

"Lions are more intelligent than some men," he said, "and more courageous than most. A lion will fight for what he has and for what he needs; he is contemptuous of cowards and wary of his equals. But he is not afraid. You can always trust a lion to be exactly what he is—and never anything else." Then he frowned. "Except that damned lion of Elkington's."

"I'm always careful of that lion," Beryl answered, "but he's really harmless. I have seen Mrs. Elkington stroke him."

"Which proves nothing," said Clutt. "A domesticated lion is only an unnatural lion—and whatever is unnatural is untrustworthy."

Beryl did not argue with him. During other rides together, she had always asked him question after question. But she knew when to be still as well. She and her father rode the rest of the way to the Elkington farm in silence.

Like many European settlers in BEA at the beginning of the century, the Elkingtons lived in a large square house with a deep, long porch on all sides, called a verandah, that provided shade from the African sun. On this porch were riding crops and saddles, for Jim Elkington, like Clutt, was a racer of horses. Horses were, in part, the reason why Clutt had come to the Elkingtons. He had wanted to view some of Jim's thoroughbreds.

On the verandah also, however, were the marks of Mrs. Elkington: wicker chairs and a round table, dressed in a white linen tablecloth that lifted as if sighing in the hot wind. Mrs. Elkington was serving tea in a silver teapot, as if what lay all around her were not the wilds of Africa but rather the prim and proper society of England. Beryl cared nothing for tea parties with crumpets and cakes. She might have hung around the adults on the porch for a short time, not much trying to be polite. But eventually, she made her escape.

She ran, as she always did, for the fun and the adventure of it. Once more she was barefoot. Perhaps she had chucked her riding boots in the red dust beneath the Elkington verandah. She ran past a hay shed where an African servant named Bishon Singh was caring for Clutt's horse and Wee MacGregor. Bishon Singh called to Beryl in Swahili as she ran out of the farmyard, but she did not slow her pace. She crested a gray-green hill and still she ran, faster now, down its side.

And then quite suddenly, Beryl stopped running. Not more than twenty yards ahead, sunning himself in the warm grass, was Paddy. Lazily, the lion beat its black-tipped tail against the ground. Then it sniffed the air and stood. Beryl knew, because her father and *arap* Maina had taught her, to be still, to be very still. The lion was harmless. She believed that. She had seen Mrs. Elkington pat its great black mane. And yet, her father had warned her that what was unnatural was untrustworthy. Her muscles tensed. Here was her test. How well had she listened to the words of *arap* Maina? How well had she learned the lesson of the leopard and the goat?

Observe the lion's eyes, *Lakweit*, *arap* Maina had taught her a long time ago while they were hunting in the bush. The lion is thinking, and he knows that we are thinking, too.

Now Beryl stared into Paddy's yellow, tear-shaped eyes. She would not run, but she would not cower, either.

The lion is fearless and we must show him that we are without fear, too, said *arap* Maina. We must laugh at his courage and shame his thoughts.

Now Beryl began to sing a marching song of the King's African Rifles. As she sang, she took one step and then another.

Watch him as he is watching you, said *arap* Maina. He is listening! And he is thinking about what he must do next.

Slowly, still singing and still watching, Beryl inched her way in a wide circle around Paddy.

Exactly what happened next is not clear. Beryl tells one version of the story in *West with the Night*:

"What I remember most clearly of the moment that followed are three things—a scream that was barely a whisper, a blow that struck me to the ground, and, as I buried my face in my arms and felt Paddy's teeth close on the flesh of my leg, a fantastically bobbing turban that was Bishon Singh's turban, appear over the edge of the hill.

"I remained conscious, but I closed my eyes and tried not to be. It was not so much the pain as it was the sound.

"The sound of Paddy's roar in my ears . . . was an immense roar that encompassed the world and dissolved me in it."

"I shut my eyes very tight and lay still under the weight of Paddy's paws."

Bishon Singh told Beryl that he had followed her over the hill, because he knew Paddy was somewhere in the area. It was Bishon Singh who had called for help, and it

35

was Jim Elkington who arrived first, swinging a rawhide whip so that it whined in the wind.

The lion's front legs were heavy on Beryl's back. Elkington charged the lion, but he did not beat it. He distracted it. Bishon Singh told Beryl that Paddy rushed at Elkington in order to defend the "fresh meat" it had taken down. The "fresh meat," of course, was Beryl, and the lion was not about to give it up. Elkington escaped into a tree, and by then Beryl had been rescued by Bishon Singh and the other *syces* who had come running. They took her to a bed in the Elkington house, then summoned Clutt back from the stables. He had been unaware of his daughter's latest dangerous encounter.

Beryl claimed she had nearly been eaten alive and would have been if Bishon Singh had not followed her over the hill to give warning. She would retell the story years later and say that the scars from Paddy's claws and fangs still marked her legs.

But Mrs. Elkington told a different ending to the story. According to Mary Lovell, one of Beryl's biographers, Margaret Elkington wrote in her unpublished memoirs that Paddy had indeed attacked the girl. But Beryl's wounds had been "no more than 'a slight scratch.'"

Once again, in looking back on her childhood, Beryl might have exaggerated the viciousness of Paddy's attack. But even "a slight scratch" from a lion must have been a horrifying experience for a nine year old. But like Buller, Beryl had survived the attack, and, in her world of absolutes, surviving was the most important thing.

five

The Egret's Message

Kibii once told Beryl a story about death. The first man to walk on Earth was Nandi, Kibii told her. But man worried all the time about what his tomorrows would be like. And so God sent the chameleon to man with a message that all his tomorrows would be like all his yesterdays. Life would never change. Life would never end. But God also sent the egret to man with a different message. The egret's message was that one day there would be no tomorrow. Death would put an end to life.

Beryl listened carefully, as she always listened while being told a story that mattered to her. The chameleon, Kibii continued, was too slow. It stopped to catch flies to eat. The long-legged egret delivered its message to man first. And that is why all men must die, Kibii explained. It is what his people believed.

Kibii's story stuck in Beryl's memory. It was interesting, but it did not have much meaning for her. After all, she was only nine years old, and all her tomorrows were still like all her yesterdays. She was *Lakweit*. She could shoot a bow and arrow. More important, *arap* Maina had given her a spear.

To a Nandi, a spear is more than just a weapon. It is a symbol of manhood. "Without it," wrote Beryl in *West with the Night,* "he can achieve nothing—no land, no cattle, no wives." Beryl's spear was smaller and more lightweight than *arap* Maina's, but it was her own. Tied to the end were black ostrich feathers. Now in the morning when she and Buller escaped to be with *arap* Maina, she took her spear with her. In the Nandi village, outside *arap* Maina's hut, she drove the spear hard into the ground, ready to hunt wart hogs.

Before a hunt, Nandi warriors drank a liquid that was part bull's blood and part milk. They believed the drink gave them strength. Elsbeth Huxley described in her own memoir, *The Flame Trees of Thika,* how the blood was obtained. An African grabbed the bull's head and twisted the neck, squeezing with one hand so that the jugular vein swelled. Then, using an arrow ringed with a tiny block of wood, another man punctured the pulsing vein. The wooden block prevented the arrow from going in too deeply. Once the arrow was removed, the spurting blood was caught in a gourd. A simple pinch closed the wound, and the bull was released. The blood was then mixed with milk. After fermenting for a few days, the liquid thickened so that it had the texture of soft, runny cheese.

That Beryl drank the bull's blood is probably fact. Ada would not have approved, of course, but that mattered little to Beryl. On her turn inside *arap* Maina's hut, she raised the gourd to her lips and drank. Then she fell in line behind the other warriors as they trotted their skip-hop gait into the bush.

While on safari in BEA in 1908, the president of the

United States, Theodore Roosevelt, witnessed a Nandi hunt and later told of it in a book called *African Game Trails*. He wrote: "They were splendid savages, stark naked, lithe as panthers, the muscles rippling under their smooth dark skins . . . faces were proud, cruel, fearless; as they ran they moved with long springy strides . . . They carried ox-hide shields painted with strange devices . . . in [each] right hand the formidable war-spear, used both for stabbing and for throwing at close quarters. . . . Herds of game—red hartebeests and striped zebra and wild swine— fled right and left before the advance of the line."

Nandi women were not allowed to hunt with the men. Nor did Kibii accompany his father on the hunt. Until his initiation into manhood, marked by a solemn and secret circumcision ceremony, Kibii was considered a boy and must tend the cattle. But Beryl was *memsahib,* the daughter of the white man. And she ran with the Nandi warriors, following a narrow trail along the edge of the Mau Forest. She ran silently on the heels of her bare feet, for she had learned her lessons well. On the bank of the Molo River, she cupped her hands and drank the cool water. In the black muck were the hoofprints of the wart hogs that had come earlier to drink. *"Lakweit!* Bend down and look so that you may learn," *arap* Maina commanded. And she obeyed. She joined the chase when a squealing baby hog had been routed. She clutched her spear fiercely as the tall grass before her parted, and a large boar, an adult, charged *arap* Maina. He planted the blade of his spear deep into the boar's vital spot. When at last the tusked animal lay dead, *arap* Maina put one foot on its tough hide and pulled free his spear and wiped it clean with a handful of grass.

These were Beryl's yesterdays—days of freedom, days when she was *Lakweit*. Perhaps if the chameleon in Kibii's story had not been so sluggish and greedy for flies, life would have continued just as it was. But the egret had delivered its message first. And Beryl's tomorrows—and Kibii's and *arap* Maina's, too—were about to change.

Miss Le May was gone. For the moment, there was no governess to discipline her. Beryl spent her time with Kibii, *arap* Maina, or in her father's stables. Or, she mounted Wee MacGregor and rode to Equator Ranch to visit Lady Delamere. Florence had become, to use Beryl's own words, "my adopted mother." More than any other woman, and especially more than Ada, Lady Delamere seemed to understand Beryl's love of freedom and the bush. Perhaps she also understood Beryl's rebellious cry for her father's attention.

Despite Lady Delamere's understanding, however, Beryl continued to act defiantly. One of Beryl's cousins remembered visiting Green Hill Farm for a short time. Together, Beryl and he killed a black momba, one of the most poisonous snakes in Africa. Beryl paraded around the farm with it stuck on a stick, waving it in the air. Another time, he watched as Beryl packed the fireplace in the living room of the big house with dry tinder. The flames that roared through the chimney like a cyclone threatened to burn the house down and fire the dry grasslands around the stables.

No doubt, Ada had had enough. In Nairobi was a

boarding school. Many children of European settlers, especially the children of those who had worked to build the Lunatic Line, lived at the school. Tuition and board were not cheap. And there was Arthur's education to be paid for as well. But Clutt agreed. He could not be with Beryl every minute to supervise her behavior. And so, in 1911, he sent Beryl away from Njoro and the only home she had ever known.

Arthur went with her to the school in Nairobi. But his presence there was little consolation. Left behind in the rondavel were the zebra skins her father had given her and her hunting spear with its tail of ostrich feathers. Left behind, too, were her father's horses and the long rides with him across the open country. Buller stayed at Njoro, of course. And Kibii as well. Beryl could no longer escape to hunt with *arap* Maina in the Mau Forest. In Nairobi, no one called her *Lakweit*. She must have felt as if she had been wrenched from everything familiar and dropped into a place where she did not belong.

In 1911, Nairobi was a city of more than 14,000 people. Buildings made of stone with red tile roofs had begun to replace the tin shanties. Rickshaws, two-wheeled carriages pulled by boys, lined the street outside the railway station. The station itself had a clock tower. Model T Ford trucks navigated the muddy roads in the rains. The town had a hospital, a few churches, a market, and a country club. The town even had electric lights. Modern civilization had come to Nairobi.

The European school was built on stilts and was located on a hill that overlooked the town. Classes began each morning at eight o'clock. Wooden desks filled the

41

room. The tops opened upward so books on English history and Latin could be stored inside. In the corner of each desk was a white porcelain ink well, and for hours on end, Beryl practiced penmanship. She had always been comfortable with African *totos*, but at school all her classmates were white. The girls wore loose-fitting dresses that buttoned at the neck and heavy, dark hose. And shoes, of course. Beryl had been around other European children before, but not often and not so constantly. She was with them all day until classes ended at five o'clock. Then, because Beryl was a boarder, she spent her time after school with the students as well. Some of her classmates thought her long, blonde hair and blue eyes beautiful. In her rondavel in Njoro, Beryl had had no mirror—she did not even have glass windows! And so it is unlikely that she had ever paid much attention to how she looked. More often than not, her hair had been tangled and coated with dust from the bush. But she had always held her head high, proudly, the way the Kipsigis did. In Nairobi, some of her fellow students interpreted Beryl's erect posture as coolness toward them.

Others in the school viewed her as a tomboy. During recess, she was always running and jumping over things. She ignored playing games with girls and preferred instead the more aggressive boys' sports, like cricket. As her biographer Errol Tryzbinski noted, Beryl purposely did things to start trouble in school, just as she had at home. One day, she rearranged the wooden desks in the room to create a sort of racetrack and then demanded that the other students run the course as if they were horses.

In *West with the Night*, Beryl wrote nothing about her

time away from Njoro at school. It was as if it had never happened. In fact, she was not at school very long. Just as she had fled from Ada and Miss Le May, Beryl ran away from school. Trzebinski stated that a student told on her and so the teachers at the school found Beryl out and brought her back. The incident resulted in Beryl's expulsion.

Which, of course, was exactly what Beryl had wanted.

She had not been away from Njoro very long. But in that short time her tomorrows had begun to change. She and Kibii were growing older. Soon he would participate in that most secret of all African ceremonies—his circumcision. Then he would be given a new name and become a man, a warrior. His would be a position forever forbidden to Beryl. It did not matter that she had drunk the blood of the bull or had her own spear with ostrich feathers. In her African world of absolutes, either you were male or female, *murani* or *memsahib*. Kibii would grow into a *murani*, a warrior. But Beryl—the *memsahib*—would simply grow up.

Other things in Beryl's life were changing as well. In 1913, Lady Delamere, who was just thirty-eight years old, died. She had been ill for some time, and rumors had circulated that she was suffering from a nervous breakdown. The immediate cause of her death was determined to be heart failure. Of all the women who were a part of Beryl's life, Lady Delamere was the only one about whom she wrote in her memoir *West with the Night*. Not even Beryl's mother, Clara, is mentioned in the book.

Clara was still living in England. Beryl had not heard from her mother for years. But in 1913, the same year that

Lady Delamere died, Clara finally divorced Clutt and married Harry Kirkpatrick, an English gentleman she had met while she was still living as Clutt's wife in Njoro. Rumors suggested that Kirkpatrick was the real reason Clara had abandoned Clutt and Beryl so many years ago. Soon after the divorce was announced, Beryl learned that Clutt and Ada intended to marry.

Kibii was maturing, leaving Beryl behind. Lady Delamere was dead. Ada was now likely to become Beryl's stepmother. Kibii's story of the chameleon and the egret suddenly became more meaningful. Beryl's yesterdays were gone. Although she was back home, she was more alone than ever. But at least she still had Buller. And she had something else—Camciscan.

"To an eagle or to an owl or to a rabbit, man must seem a masterful and yet a forlorn animal;" she wrote in *West with the Night,* "he has but two friends . . . the dog and the horse."

Camciscan arrived at Njoro in the early morning. His reputation arrived before the train had even pulled into the railway station. He was a bay stallion that had won the English Derby, and Clutt had purchased him and brought him to Africa to stud his own stable of racing horses. The door of the stable car slid open and a ramp was put in place. A *syce* led the stallion from the rail car out into the cold morning air of the highlands. The animal shook his body. His hooves were on solid ground at last after weeks of being stabled in a rolling ship and then a swaying, dusty train. But the highlands with its thin, icy air and peppery red dust was quite unlike that softer, greener place Camciscan had left behind. If it is possible for a horse to remember and to feel emotion—and Beryl would have said a horse could—then Camciscan must have felt as if he, too, had been wrenched from all that was familiar and dropped into a place where he wasn't sure he belonged.

He stamped and flared his nostrils anxiously as a circle of Africans stood admiring him. They said his name, and Beryl repeated it out loud, "Camciscan." Clutt stepped forward and put his hand on the stallion's neck, pleased with his purchase. Beryl moved closer then, too. Camciscan snorted at her, but she was not afraid. She took the reins and led the horse along the dirt road back to her father's stables.

In remembering the morning that Camciscan arrived at the farm, Beryl described herself as being "foolishly happy." Once again, it is a bit of mystery to know for certain how old she was that day. Birthdays did not matter to a girl who never celebrated them with cake and candles, whose father most likely added another year for her in his black book just as he measured her height in years with a piece of charcoal etched into the wall beside the fireplace. Age did not matter. The horse did.

Beryl knew horses. She spent hours every day grooming them and exercising them. It is not unusual then that she would describe herself as if she were a horse, as well. Her legs, for example, she said were long and lanky, "like a colt's." Perhaps when she looked at Camciscan that first day and all the days after, Beryl saw something of herself in the wild stallion. He dug his hoof in the dirt, snorted, and bared his teeth to warn others away. Beryl was rebellious, too. Once she had

45

planted spiders and snakes in Ada's bed to drive her away.

But Beryl shared something more with Camciscan: loneliness and a mistrust of others. She saw it in the stallion's eyes and in the way he stepped away from her whenever she entered his stall to shovel out the manure and replace the urine-soiled straw with fresh bedding. Years later, in writing about Camciscan in *West with the Night*, she slipped inside his stallion skin and imagined how she must have appeared to him. She wrote: "Mornings came when Camciscan waited for the girl with his ears and with his eyes, because he had learned the sound of her bare feet on the ground. . . . In time he found himself getting used to the girl, but he would not let it be more than that. He could feel that she was trying to break through the loneliness that he lived by, and he remembered the reasons there were to mistrust men."

Surely Beryl had her own reasons to mistrust people. Her mother had abandoned her. Her father did not have enough time to give her. Ada and the other European women were trying to mold her into being someone she could never be. In writing about Camciscan, Beryl could have been writing about herself.

"He did not like a hand with a tremor. He did not trust the smell of a man that had nothing of the earth in it nor any sweat in it." That, too, was like Beryl. "He sometimes felt the urge to move closer . . . but the loneliness of which he was so proud never permitted this."

Camciscan was a powerful horse for a grown man to handle. But Beryl also rode him. One day while riding through the valley, the stallion threw her. Beryl struck her head against a tree and lay there unconscious until some-one—Clutt or one of the *syces*— found her. Her head was bloody. The *syces* carried her back to the house. She suffered a concussion. Ada had had some nursing experience, and so quite likely she cared for Beryl. For seven days, the girl lay in her bed. Once she had recovered, however, she did not shy away from Camciscan's stall. Once again, she padded barefoot into the stables. Once again, she pitchforked the soiled straw out of the stall. And once again, the stallion inched away from her into the corner.

One day as she worked on his hooves, digging out the caked red dirt, he turned to watch her. All at once, he bared his teeth and bit hard into her back. Beryl remembered being shaken like a rug and then falling against the stable wall. She huddled on the floor. "A thoroughbred stallion with anger in his eyes is not a sight to entrance anyone but a novice," she would one day write. "If you are aware of the power and the speed and the intelligence in that towering symmetrical body, you will hold your breath. . . . You will know that the teeth of a horse can crush a bone, that hooves can crush a man."

Beryl held her breath. But Camciscan's anger was now spent. He did not trample her.

But a stallion's fear or anger can surge at anytime and mount into madness. Again, while Beryl was riding Camciscan in the valley, the horse stopped dead. Beryl kicked him hard in the side, commanding him forward. She would not be dominated by him. Nor would Camciscan give in to her. The stallion reared, trying to fling her off his back. Beryl's knees and legs pressed hard against his body and she held on tight. All the while, her whip whistled and stung against his hindquarters. When he twisted his head to bite her legs, she whipped his muzzle. She could have leapt from his back, but her father had taught her—no, had warned her—never to let go of the reins.

"You do not abandon a horse to his fury," she wrote. "You do not throw away the rules. You hang on—and tremble."

Again Camciscan reared and pawed the air, then bucked and whirled swiftly in the dust, and still Beryl hung on. The horse raised himself on his hind legs and threw his head and neck back and, losing his balance, fell hard against the ground. Somehow, Beryl managed to escape being crushed by the stallion's body.

The fall broke the stallion's tantrum. When the dust had settled, Beryl was still holding the reins tight. Free now of his madness, Camciscan shuddered and allowed Beryl to touch tenderly all the painful places she had made with her whip.

"Horses are not tamed by whips or by blows," she wrote. To tame Camciscan was not the reason why she had whipped him. Beryl respected Camciscan's arrogance. It was bred in him, and she did not try to beat it out of him. He could not help being what he was—a thoroughbred, a stallion. She understood that.

Beryl believed that in time Camciscan came to understand some things about her, as well—that she was his equal, a thoroughbred, too; and that she loved him.

six

The Horse with Wings

During the summer of 1914, when Beryl was not quite twelve years old, her world changed again, dramatically.

"My father's face had become more grave than it had ever been before," Beryl wrote, "and the voices of the men he spoke with were sombre. There was a lot of head-shaking and talk about gloomy, schoolbookish places that had nothing to do with Africa."

It all began with a murder. It had happened not in Africa but rather half a world away on another continent in a city called Sarajevo. Sarajevo was the capital of a territory in Europe called Bosnia-Hercegovina. A few years earlier, a powerful dual-monarchy, Austria and Hungary, had claimed the Bosnia-Hercegovina territory as its own. While visiting Sarajevo on June 28, 1914, Archduke Francis Ferdinand, the heir to the throne of Austria-Hungary, and his wife were assassinated by a man who opposed the Austro-Hungarian rule.

Surely one country declaring war on another thousands of miles away could not affect the lives of the

European settlers in the highlands. Many settlers in British East Africa had never heard of the Archduke. But within weeks, tremors from the Archduke's murder had shaken all of Europe. Before summer was over, eight nations and seventeen million men had been drawn into a war that would be unlike any the world had ever seen before. Years later, historians would call the terrible conflict World War I.

Germany was sympathetic to the Austro-Hungarian cause and began to mobilize troops against Russia and France. On August 4, Great Britain stepped into the fray as an ally of France and Russia and declared war on Germany. Suddenly the terrible events of that summer did not seem so far away anymore. Germany, like Great Britain, had colonies in East Africa. German territory, referred to as GEA, bordered the British Protectorate to the south. Majestic Kilimanjaro was, in fact, in German East Africa. In just six weeks, the ripple effects of the Archduke's assassination had crossed the Indian Ocean and reached Africa's shores.

The British government that controlled BEA was ill-prepared for war. The King's African Rifles had about sixty British officers and fewer than 2,000 trained soldiers, most of whom were *askaris,* or African guards. Nor was the army equipped with artillery or gas masks or the heavier machines of war—tanks, planes, or guns that fired shells over trenches. A few Model T trucks had guns mounted on them, but the moving parts were old and often jammed. But war had been declared just the same, and the response of the European settlers was immediate and enthusiastic. Men left their wives behind to manage

the coffee plantations and farms
in Nairobi with what horses and gu
save the Protectorate should the fighting
"proper" war. Especially important was keep
Snake free of German sabotage for the railway wa
and blood of the white settlement. The men who e
ed, however, made up a rag-tag army. Their uniforms were
mismatched and not particularly military. Some men
wore khaki shorts; others wore trousers. Some wore boots;
others did not. Their sleeveless bush jackets and pith hel-
mets or cloth terai hats dressed with ostrich plumes
seemed more suitable for safari than for combat.

The new recruits organized into squadrons, each
squadron carrying a banner on a bamboo pole. Armed
with their elephant rifles and bushman's knives and
mules weighed down with blankets, pots, and water jugs,
the soldiers paraded on review in Nairobi for the governor
of the Protectorate. As they marched off to war, the men
sang a cheerful song:

> *Hooray! Hooray! We're off to GEA*
> *Hooray! Hooray! The squareheads we will slay,*
> *And so we sing this happy song*
> *Upon this happy day*
> *As we go marching to Tabora.*

No doubt they thought they could make a quick game
of it. But they were wrong. The fighting would last for six
years and become known as The Great War. In Africa
alone, more than 50,000 men, both white and black,
would die.

ı enlisted in the
ınor. But he was a
ρear is everything.
with the others, he
ɔlack's man spear. To
was killed in German
s body where he had

se with Wings
while they congregated
s they had, ready to
r develop into a
ng the Iron
the life
ist-

:ath must have stunned
Beryl. ᴜ.   . a person who mattered
very much to heı. _   ɔngeance. "When I am cir-
cumcised and become a ıı. ani," Kibii said, and drink
blood and curdled milk like a man. . . . I will find whoev-
er it was that killed my father and put my spear in his
heart."

"You are very selfish, Kibii," Beryl said. "I can jump as
high as you can. . . . I can throw a spear almost as far. We
will find him together and put both our spears in his
heart."

But war is a faceless battle, and it was a child's grief
that vowed vengeance. *Arap* Maina was only one of so
many who had died and who were dying still. As the
fighting continued, the government required women and
children who had been left unprotected in the highlands
to leave. Some moved to Nairobi. Others, like Elspeth
Huxley, left the country altogether. Production on the
plantations and on the farms came almost to a standstill.
The same was true on Green Hill Farm.

Before The Great War, Nakuru had been just a small
village in the highlands approximately twenty miles from

The Horse with Wings

Lord Delamere's Equator Ranch. Delamere had built and still owned a small hotel in the village there. The hotel accommodated the settlers who traveled to Nakuru to show and to auction off their livestock. A racetrack and a school had recently been built. Once The Great War had erupted, however, Nakuru became an important army outpost. The government of the Protectorate had conscripted thousands of mules and horses, including some of Clutt's own thoroughbreds, for use by the East African Mounted Rifles. Clutt did not enlist to fight, but he volunteered his services to work with the horses at Nakuru.

Ada also volunteered. Like many of the white women settlers, she nursed the wounded, and Green Hill Farm became a sort of rehabilitation center for officers recovering from battle. Many of the officers served in calvary units and brought their wounded horses to Clutt's farm, as well. Beryl claimed that she had always had a phobia about sickness and disease, that she could more calmly face a deadly black momba or a python than a person suffering from malaria or blackwater fever. But her phobia seemed not to include animals. A wounded or diseased dog or horse she cared for tenderly, without any repulsion.

One such horse was Baron. He belonged to an officer, whom Beryl referred to only as Dennis, who had come to Green Hill Farm to recuperate from a gruesome face wound. Baron had been badly injured in the fighting. For nights, Beryl slept in the stable with the horse. When Baron had recovered sufficiently, she took him on rides across the valley. Dennis sometimes rode alongside her. He taught her how to shoot a revolver. But the war had not ended for Dennis or Baron. Once fully recov-

53

ered, both horse and officer returned to the fighting. Would Baron survive the shelling and bullets this time? Beryl wondered. She was not hopeful. Her hatred of the war—already fueled by *arap* Maina's death—had grown. Death was a natural part of living. Africa and its abundant wildlife had taught her that. In Africa, the death of one creature gave life to another. War, on the other hand, was a senseless slaughter. And, it seemed to Beryl, endless.

Another officer who found his way to Green Hill Farm to rest and recuperate was Captain Alexander Purves—called Jock by his friends. He had not been shot or gassed, but was suffering from dysentery, a disease he had most likely contracted by eating contaminated water or food on the battlefront. When he arrived at Njoro in 1916, Beryl was not quite fourteen years old. Quite likely during the six weeks that Jock stayed at the farm, he watched Beryl as she worked in her father's stables and rode his racehorses, including the powerful Camciscan. As she had with the other officers, Beryl sometimes went riding with Jock. She thought him "a nice man," strong and athletic though his illness had weakened him. In Beryl's eyes, Captain Purves was just another soldier.

Jock, however, was immediately attracted to Beryl. She was tall with long legs and slim hips. She was strong, a good shot with a bow and arrow, and absolutely fearless in the way she handled her father's horses. Physically, she was maturing into a beautiful woman, but at fourteen she was still considered a child, and Jock could not act upon his feelings for her. At thirty years old, he was more than twice her age. There was also the war. Like the other officers who had come to Green Hill, Captain Purves must return to the fighting.

Before he left, Jock might have struck a deal with Clutt. According to Trzebinski, Jock had fallen in love with Beryl at first sight and asked Clutt if he could marry her when Beryl turned eighteen, the legal age in BEA for a white woman to marry. In exchange for the promise of marrying Beryl, Jock would pay the tuition and boarding fees for Beryl to attend a private school in Nairobi. Once the war had ended and Beryl was old enough, Jock would make her his wife.

There may be some truth to the story, for the war had pinched Clutt's finances, and it is unlikely that he would have had the extra money at that time for Beryl's education. Whether the story is true or not, Clutt sent Beryl away from Njoro for the second time. In 1916, she became a student once again, this time in a school run by Miss Blanche Secombe. The school was located on the hill near the military hospital in Nairobi. Many of the other students had come to the school from upcountry, as Beryl had. Like her, they were used to the freedom of open spaces. Many missed riding their horses and resented the matronly teachers in their high-necked, starched dresses.

Once again, Beryl was living in a dormitory with eight other girls, and although she was like them in some ways, she was not very well liked by most of them. Once again, it could have been her striking good looks. Or it might have been her coolness toward them. She was often quiet and still, as if she wanted nothing to do with them. Beryl was not used to having girlfriends and did not primp in front of a mirror or chatter about herself. She was a loner.

But even a loner needs someone to talk to once in a while.

Doris Waterman lived in the dormitory with Beryl. Her father owned the New Stanley Hotel in Nairobi. She was not jealous of Beryl's good looks or put off by her occasional coolness. She enjoyed Beryl's disruptions in the classroom and often got in trouble herself for joining in Beryl's antics. "Dos" became Beryl's first true friend. They spent all their free time together and often stole time, skipping class or escaping from the dormitory. They walked past the rows of hospital tents to the cemetery and continued onto the Athi Plains. Beryl would have liked to have kept walking, one hundred miles all the way back to Njoro.

She did return to Green Hill Farm for holidays, but they were always short visits. One holiday, she invited Dos to come home with her, but the Watermans refused. Clutt and Ada were not yet married, and Beryl's home was not a proper home for a young girl, Dos's family felt, even to visit. That Beryl felt close to Dos is proven by the fact that she told her some private things about herself, things she did not tell the others. Her real mother had left her, Beryl admitted. Ada was horribly unkind to her. And she drank! But Beryl never spoke ill of her father.

Beryl was older, but no less rebellious and no more interested in studying than she had ever been. One day, she mounted her bicycle and simply left. Other students, unhappy at a school they thought was more like a prison, followed her. The matrons accused Beryl of encouraging the others to run away from school. She was a bad influence and the end result was expulsion. Again.

Clutt welcomed her back. What choice did he have? But never again would he hire a governess or send Beryl to school in the hopes of giving her a proper British education. The teachers and the schools had failed. Perhaps to acknowledge that he had lost and Beryl had won, he built a house for her. The three-room cottage had cedar floors and glass windows. Clutt furnished it with tables, chairs, books, even a mirror. Beryl loved the cottage, and the living arrangements—Ada in one house and Beryl in another—apparently pleased Clutt, as well.

Once more, Beryl's life was caring for her father's horses. In this, she excelled. The *syces* who worked in the stables knew that Beryl's word was as good as Clutt's. If she gave a command, they obeyed. If she was not happy with the way a *syce* had treated her father's horses or if a *syce* failed to do the work she expected of him, she—not Clutt—fired him. Clutt came to rely more and more on her skills as he himself was busy racing his horses, including Camciscan, and winning.

"I do not know why most foals are born at night," Beryl wrote in *West with the Night*, "but most of them are."

On a November night in 1917, one of Clutt's thoroughbred mares named Coquette was about to foal. Clutt was away, busy with some other task. Perhaps he was at the mill, making ready a supply of wood-fuel for the army. Or he could have been at Nakuru. As she moved Coquette into the foaling room, Beryl looked closely at the mare. Her eyes were dull. Her head was heavy, and her body, shapeless. She felt the mare's ears for fever.

Coquette was healthy and strong, but the labor ahead of her would be painful.

Beryl lay her head against Coquette's heavy belly and felt the movement of the unborn foal. It would come tonight, but not yet. She told Toombo, one of Clutt's *syces*, to call her when it was time. Then she and Buller left the stables and returned to her cottage.

Minutes earlier in the foaling box, she had stared into the eyes of the pregnant mare. Now, in her cottage, Beryl gazed into the mirror at her own reflection. Blue eyes, thin lips, a long, oval face, hair bleached by the sun—she must have thought her image disappointing somehow, for she wrote about that moment: "I have always known what I looked like—but at fifteen-odd, I become curious to know what can be done about it. Nothing, I suppose— and who would there be to know the difference? Still, at that age few things can provoke more wonderment than a mirror."

What connection between herself and Coquette was Beryl searching for in the mirror? About Coquette, she wondered what sort of life the mare would bring into the world. Would the foal's "new heart be strong and stubborn enough" to survive? Would it "have the anger to feed and to grow and to demand its needs?" Looking in the mirror in her cottage while she waited for Toombo to tell her that Coquette's time had come, Beryl might have asked the same questions about herself. Was she strong and stubborn enough to survive, to demand what she needed to be happy? Or perhaps she was simply wondering what many fifteen-year-old girls wonder when they look at themselves in a mirror: Am I pretty?

Will anyone love me? Does anyone care?

Toombo came to the cottage door. "Come quickly, Beru," he said. Beryl hurried back to the stables.

In the dim light of the hurricane lamp, Beryl saw Coquette lying on her side in the foaling box. "Horses are not voiceless in pain," Beryl wrote. The mare panted, grunted, and jerked. Beryl knelt beside her. The mare's labored breathing slowed and was almost calm again. But soon the pains and the panting began again. Instinct was commanding Coquette. Instinct had told her to lie down. Beryl was only the midwife. She could do nothing for the mare except wait with her. Finally, one agonized cry told Beryl and Toombo the waiting was over. Toombo turned up the wick in the hurricane lamp so they could better see. Coquette trembled. Beryl moved into position and saw the hooves, encased in the transparent birthing sac.

Now Beryl slipped her hands around the unborn foal's thin legs. When instinct commanded the mare's muscles to push, Beryl responded, too, pulling gently but firmly. She reached in, higher up, and pulled again as Coquette pushed. Slowly the nose appeared. Another push and the head appeared. Then, with a final agonized effort, the body encased in the slippery sac was born into Beryl's arms.

Instinct had not taught Beryl what she must do next. She had learned it by watching and assisting at other births. The foal had not yet taken its first breath of cold, highland air. It could not until Beryl freed it from the birthing sac. This she did quickly. Then using twine from the foaling kit, she tied the umbilical cord. Next she reached for the knife and sliced through the fleshy cord. At once, blood flowed onto the hay. Beryl doused the cut with antiseptic. Freed now from her heavy burden, Coquette clamored to her feet again. Curiously, she sniffed her wet foal. Then, reassured, she used her tongue to clean the remains of the birthing sac from the newborn.

Beryl stood, too. Grinning, she turned to look for Toombo, but saw instead her father.

"So there you are," he said.

She had not heard Clutt enter the foaling room, but she realized at once that he must have been standing behind her for some time. He had not spoken or interfered, but he had watched her do what had to be done. Beryl must have held her breath as she stared into her father's dark eyes. Would he approve or disapprove of her?

It was not the first time that Clutt had witnessed the birth of an animal, especially one of his thoroughbreds. But that November night Beryl said she saw "bright interest in his eyes—as if, after all these years, he has at last seen the birth of a foal!"

"A fine job of work and a fine colt," he said. "Shall I reward you or Coquette—or both?"

Toombo grinned. Beryl said nothing.

"Render unto Caesar," said Clutt. "You brought him to life. He shall be yours."

The colt was hers. Hers.

It was the greatest gift that her father could have given her, much greater than a cottage with cedar shingles and a mirror inside. Horses were what Clutt knew best and loved most. Now he had given one of his prized thoroughbreds to her. Her father was not a man to show or speak of his love. On that November night, he had expressed it in a way that did not require words. Beryl slipped her arm around him, and for a while longer they stood, linked together, and watched her colt struggle to stand on its wobbly legs.

It was a perfect colt, Beryl thought. And though it was not yet beautiful, one day it would be. She called the colt Pegasus, remembering a Greek myth her father had once told her about a horse with wings.

It was a perfect moment, too, between parent and child. For never again would Beryl and her father be as close as this shared triumph.

seven

Losing Njoro

When the war ended in 1918, Jock returned to Njoro and purchased 600 acres of land. More than two years had passed since he had first seen Beryl riding her father's horses, and Jock's feelings for her had not changed. Still, for another year more, Clutt withheld his permission for Beryl to marry. Then in August 1919, he finally agreed to announce the engagement. Beryl was sixteen. Jock was thirty-three.

Beryl's future husband was more than six feet tall, handsome, and athletic. Born in England to a family with some wealth and social standing, he had become a sports hero on the rugby field while still a teenager. As an officer during The Great War, he had distinguished himself. No doubt, Clutt thought Jock would be a good influence on Beryl. If governesses could not control her, perhaps Jock could.

Beryl knew very little about the duties expected of a wife. She had grown up observing wild animals in the bush and caring for the domesticated animals on the farm. She understood that sexual intercourse and the births that resulted from it were a natural part of living. It was the long-term commitment of marriage vows that Beryl did not comprehend.

Clutt and Ada had been living together for years as if they were husband and wife, but Beryl had long ago refused to acknowledge her father's mistress as anything but an unneeded—and in Beryl's eyes, an unwanted—servant. The teachers at the English schools in Nairobi had not taught Beryl what a wife's role should be. Or if they had, Beryl ignored the lessons. She knew something about the wives of the Masai, though. They wore thick coils of jewelry, often weighing more than one pound, in their earlobes. The heavy coils proclaimed to all that they were married women, and they never allowed their husbands to see them without their jewelry.

Then there was Jebbta. The wife of *arap* Maina wore ankle-length skins and mixed bark brew for her husband. She avoided the eyes of the men and was shy around them. A Nandi wife never jumped or wrestled, and she most definitely did not hunt. Beryl could never accept being the sort of subservient wife a Masai or a Nandi woman was expected to be.

Clutt formally announced his daughter's engagement at the Coming-out Turf Ball held in August in Nairobi. Coming-out meant being introduced to society. It marked the passage from girlhood to womanhood. Even in the highlands of East Africa, the British settlers continued the tradition. Clutt, Ada, and Beryl traveled to Nairobi for the ball and booked rooms in the New Stanley Hotel. Beryl's friend Dos also attended the event. According to Trzebinski, Dos recalled that Beryl had to share a room with Ada. The two argued over Beryl's clothes, Dos said. Beryl thought the dress Ada had selected for her was too "frilly." For Beryl's hair, Ada insisted that she wear a "wreath of rosebuds." Beryl hated the costume and wore it grudgingly.

In the weeks that followed the Turf Ball, plans for the wedding continued. Where to hold the reception was a bit of a problem. The Muthaiga Club was too expensive, for Clutt's farm was slipping deeper and deeper into debt. But there was another reason to avoid the country club. Clutt and Ada were still not married, and the "committee" that oversaw the management of the club had rules about "immoral" behavior. Ada chose the Norfolk Hotel instead, located on the outskirts of Nairobi. Its inner flagstone courtyard would be a charming place for a wedding party. It is likely that it was Ada, not Beryl, who also wrote up the wedding list, selected the bride's dress and bouquet, and arranged for the military band of the KAR to play at the hotel reception.

Beryl would not be seventeen until October, and so she was not legally old enough to marry. But August was the month that horses in East Africa were aged. Possibly Clutt had added one or even two strikes to Beryl's age in his black leather book. On the marriage certificate, her age is recorded as eighteen years, and it was witnessed as fact by Lord Delamere.

On October 15, Jock married Beryl in All Saints Church in Nairobi. Beryl wore a dress of ivory satin with pearl trimmings, another frilly frock. At the door of the church, she linked her arm through her father's and, inches taller than he, walked up the aisle to where Jock waited. Clutt gave him her hand.

The wedding was a local society event, for Charles Clutterbuck's racing colors of black and yellow were well-known in Nairobi. An article about the wedding appeared in the *East African Standard*. The reception was "largely attended," the newspaper reported, with many of Jock's "brother officers" seated in the church pews. The newspaper also reported that the bride wore a tailored white suit as she and her husband left for a honeymoon in India where Jock's family was living.

A satin wedding gown with a veil of white silk and a tailored suit—this was the dress expected of a bride and a wife. But Beryl had always been more comfortable in khaki shorts or riding breeches, without a hat and often without even shoes. It would not be long before Beryl would revert back to her old clothing and her old ways.

In October in the highlands of East Africa, the short rains begin. The rain may fall for days at a time, but soon the sky is clear and blue again. Then in January and February, the Great Rift Valley becomes hot and dry. The sun bleaches the color from the sky and from the land. Heat rises in transparent flames. "I had never before seen heat, as you can see smoke or rain," wrote Elspeth Huxley. "But there it was, jigging and quavering above the brown grasses and spiky thorn-trees."

In March, clouds knot overhead, and the wind rustles through the dusty trees, sounding like rain. But the long rains do not begin until the end of the month. These spring rains are heavy and continuous through June.

A typical equatorial storm, wrote Beryl, was "instantaneous, violent, and all-encompassing. It made the world black, then split the blackness with knives of light. It made the great trees creak and the bamboos moan. Forest hogs ran for cover, terrified parrots darted in green and scarlet arcs through the lightning." What were a few pools of mud became a river again. What was brown and burnt and bone-dry sprouted green and fresh with new life.

In March of 1919, however, the rains failed.

The war was over, but another battle for life had begun. The drought continued throughout the year, and the settlers watched helplessly as their crops curled and yellowed. Across the Rift Valley, the thorn trees blackened. Swamps dried to caked mud, and wildlife died of thirst. In the sky, vultures circled soundlessly.

"All the seeds died one year at Njoro and on all the farms around Njoro," Beryl wrote in *West with the Night*. "The sky was clear as a window one morning. It was so the next morning, and the next, and on every morning that followed until it was hard to remember how rain felt, or how a field looked, green and moist with life so that a naked foot sank into it."

Beryl knew that the drought was turning the Great Rift Valley into stone. She knew, too, that when the seeds die, the mill has no grain to grind, and so the mill dies, too. But apparently Beryl did not realize how deeply in debt her father had become. He sat now for long hours at his desk in the big house, his regular pint of beer on the table beside him, working the numbers in his books. His business was to buy grain for a certain amount of money, grind it in his mill, then sell it for a higher price. But in

1920, a year after Beryl's marriage to Jock Purves, Clutt could no longer make the numbers add up in his favor.

"We sat for an hour in his little study," Beryl remembered, "and he spoke to me more seriously than he ever had done before. His arm lay across the big black book that was closed now and he told me many things I had never known."

He told her about the contracts he had signed with the government and with other vendors to sell his ground meal to them at a fixed price. But the drought had increased the cost of the corn and the wheat he must buy. It was simple arithmetic. Although Beryl had hated school and had endured Miss Le May's rhino whip rather than do her numbers properly, she was not stupid. Clutt was broke.

But what he told her next must have stunned her. He was selling Green Hill Farm. He had no choice. The mill, the big house, the stables—yes, even the horses—no longer belonged to him. Everything, right down to the wheelbarrows, must be auctioned off in order to satisfy the bank debts. Clutt was not just broke; he was bankrupt.

To Beryl, her father had always been a powerful man, much more a hero to her than Jock had ever been on the rugby field or the battlefield. After more than fifteen years of back-breaking work, chiseling the farm and the mill out of the thorny bush and the cedar forest, Clutt had lost it all. He was powerless to save Green Hill Farm. Errol Trzebinski says that Beryl felt ashamed of him and of their dire situation. But in *West with the Night,* Beryl described her father as a man of honor who would not stoop so low as to welch on his signed contracts. Once he gave his word, he stuck to it. She did not blame him for the drought or for any bad decisions that might have resulted in his heavy debts. She described him as being concerned mostly for her own future.

We have to think what to do next, her father said.

He had already thought about what he and Ada would do. They were leaving East Africa. He had found a position as a horse trainer in Peru in South America. This was perhaps the most devastating news for Beryl. Peru was the other side of the world. She was losing not only the farm but her father also.

According to Beryl, Clutt asked her to go with him to Peru. "He wanted me to come," she wrote.

But once again, when it comes to Beryl's relationship with her father, the waters are muddy. Neither of Beryl's biographers—Trzebinski or Lovell—state clearly that Clutt wanted Beryl to join him. Given the years of hostility between his daughter and Ada, including the need for separate living arrangements at Green Hill Farm, it seems unlikely that Clutt would have asked his daughter to come. Besides, she was a married woman, living with her husband, and his farm was financially secure. Clutt had given her away at the altar. Beryl's place was with Jock, not him.

That night, Beryl asked her father if he thought she could become a trainer of racehorses, as he had been.

It was not an easy question to answer.

Horse racing was a man's sport. No woman had yet received a trainer's license under English Jockey Club rules. But then, Beryl was no ordinary woman. *Arap* Maina had taught her to be fearless. Kibii had taught her to be competitive. Clutt had taught her how to manage horses and to think like them. Although she was not yet eighteen years old, she had years of valuable experience in her father's stables. The Clutterbuck name was still worth something, even if the farm was not. But even if she got her trainer's license, she would still need to win the confidence of the owners. Somehow she would have to persuade them to bring their thoroughbreds to her, a woman not quite eighteen years old; to trust that despite her sex and her young age she could train their mares and stallions as her father had into winners on the racetrack.

Beryl was courageous and independent enough to try it. What people thought of her had never deterred her from doing what she wanted to do. But, she asked her father, was she "expert enough" with horses to actually succeed?

His answer was cautious. She still had much to learn. Clutt advised her to go to the stables at Molo, where she might find someone willing to take a chance on her. "Work and hope," he told her. "But never hope more than you work."

The newspapers were full of it. Clutterbuck was ruined. He was leaving racing and Africa. And all his fine horses were going on the block.

On December 11, 1920, the auctioneers came from Nakuru and made an inventory of everything to be sold at Green Hill Farm. In addition to the house and the stables, and all the furnishings and gear, nearly fifty horses were on the list, including the regal Camciscan. The first horse auction was held soon after on December 14. Beryl was not present that day to witness her childhood being sold off to the highest bidder. On Camciscan's turn, the numbers soared. The stallion was eight years old and had sired many foals. Where other horses in Clutt's stables sold for seventy-five, eighty, and 130 British pounds, the bid for Camciscan jumped into the hundreds. When the auctioneer's hammer finally came down, Camciscan had been sold for 760 pounds to Lord Delamere. To learn that Camciscan was going to the stables of a close friend must have been some comfort to Beryl.

Pegasus was the only horse not for sale. He still belonged to Beryl. But Jock bid on and won two more horses on the auction block. One was a yearling called Breach of Promise that he bought for forty pounds. The mare's name and age were symbolic of Jock and Beryl's relationship. When Jock had married Beryl, a rumor circulated that he had won her hand by offering to erase a large debt Clutt owed him. Jock had bid on Beryl, the gossips said, and won her rather cheaply. By the time of Clutt's bankruptcy, the yearling marriage had already begun to sour. Both Beryl and Jock had made a breach of promise to each other. While Beryl might not have understood or accepted the duties expected of her as a wife, neither did Jock understand Beryl's love of freedom and her need to cut her own path in the world. Although they lived together as husband and wife, she flirted openly with other men. Jock was possessive and jealous, and when he drank, often abusive.

Change and chance go hand-in-hand. One sparks the other. The changes in Beryl's life—her failing marriage, the loss of the farm and her father—now forced her to take a chance. She was not afraid of risk. Her father had shaped his own life by risk-taking—leaving familiar England for the unseen highlands of East Africa, building a mill, racing horses. So what if he ultimately had failed? There was no shame in that. The shame was in not trying. Now it was Beryl's turn to try.

After the second horse auction, Beryl applied for and received her trainer's license under English Jockey Club rules. She was the first woman to do so, not just in East Africa but also in England. That was the easy part. She heeded her father's advice to never hope more than she worked. Dressed once more in long pants and a loose shirt and leather moccasins, Beryl went to work. She was determined to succeed and, by succeeding, to win back her father's soiled reputation.

Her first horses were not the sleek and satiny steeds that had made the Clutterbuck racing colors famous in the winner's circle. Her father had left her a filly that had not drawn a high enough bid at auction—Reve D'Or was a horse that apparently no one wanted. In addition, the horses Jock had bought were dull animals compared to Pegasus and Camiscan. But these were all the horses she had. She hired a jockey named Walters to work with her. And so it was at eighteen that Beryl began her racing career.

Major Mac Conduitt was a veteran of The Great War and a friend of Jock's. At the December auction, Mac had bid on Cam, a two year old sired by Camciscan. Soon after, he brought the horse to Beryl for training. Cam would be Beryl's first test. She worked with the horse for weeks, right through the rainy season. Then on June 25, under her new racing colors of blue and gold, she entered the horse in the trial stakes at Nakuru. Cam was untried, meaning he had never officially raced before. Beryl pinned her future on him. The son of Camiscan did not fail her. At the gun, he broke from the gate, took the lead, and held it. The other horses simply could not catch him. The newspaper reported that the trainer of the winning horse was Mr. B. Purvis. The name was misspelled and the gender was wrong, but it was a good beginning nevertheless.

"Trainers, big chested; trainers, flat chested; all of them men," she wrote. "All of them older than my eighteen years. Full of being men. Confident. Cocksure. They have a right to be. They know what they know, some of which I have still to learn, but not much I think. Not much I hope. We shall see. We shall see."

eight

The Decents

B eryl was working hard to prove her worth in a man's game—horseracing. She was quite comfortable around men and generally preferred their company rather than the company of women. And yet one woman was to have a great influence on Beryl's life. She was Karen Dinesen. In 1914, at the age of twenty-eight, she had left her home in Denmark and emigrated to British East Africa to become the wife of her second cousin, Baron Bror Von Blixen. It was an arranged marriage. Neither the bride nor the groom were in love. Karen had arrived in BEA just before The Great War erupted. Together with her husband—whom everyone good naturedly called Blix—she began a coffee plantation in the Ngong Hills, nearly nine thousand feet above sea level and not very far from the former Clutterbuck farm in Njoro.

Soon after her arrival, however, Karen realized that Blix was neither dependable as a coffee planter nor faithful as a husband. The Baron and Baroness lived apart, mostly. He spent a great deal of time socializing at the racetrack and the Muthaiga Country Club in Nairobi or serving as a guide to the wealthy white hunters who came on safari to Kenya Colony (as BEA was now officially called). She lived at Mbogani, her house made of field stones in the Ngong Hills. The management of the coffee plantation became Karen Blixen's responsibility, and her love. Years later, the Baroness would write about her farm in the highlands, using the pen name Isak Dinesen. But that was long after she had left Africa. While she was still mistress of Mbogani, she used to play a game of classifying animals into one of two categories: the respectables and the decents. The respectables belonged to a community and served it well. Domesticated animals such as pigs and poultry and most dogs, for example, were respectables. But the decents, said Karen, "belonged to God." The community held no sway over them. Wild animals—leopards and lions and elephants—were the decents.

Karen judged people in the same way. In Denmark, very probably she had been one of the respectables. But once she found her place in the African highlands, she became a decent. "Nine thousand feet up, [I] felt safe," she wrote, and she "laughed at the ambition of the new arrivals, of the Missions, the business people, and the government itself, to make the continent of Africa respectable."

Lord Delamere had once said that he would prove East Africa was a white man's country. But Karen Blixen was not so sure it was. Africa could be settled, but it could not be tamed.

The Baroness first met Beryl during the war when the girl was still Clutt's wild child and not yet Jock Purves's teenage bride. Karen was nearly sixteen years older than

The Decents

Beryl, and so her initial relationship with her was as an adult to an undisciplined, but rather "decent" child. Perhaps even then, Karen saw in Beryl something of herself. The girl was a risk-taker.

Despite the differences in their ages, the two women had something else in common: loneliness. The eighteen years during which Karen Blixen lived in Kenya Colony were the most challenging and most eventful years of her life. Everything that happened to her afterward simply did not measure up. But in *Out of Africa,* a book she wrote long after she had left Mbogani, she admitted: "At times, life on the farm was very lonely, and in the stillness of the evenings when the minutes dripped from the clock, life seemed to be dripping out of you with them, just for want of white people to talk to." Beryl's loneliness, though, went deeper than just someone to talk to. It was rooted in her mother's abandonment and her father's preoccupation with things other than his daughter.

After the war, the relationship between Beryl and the Baroness changed. They shared something else in common now: each had a paper marriage and a husband she did not love. Yet despite their failed marriages and sometimes loneliness, both women loved the land—the sight and sounds and smells of the African highlands. It was not the land that had disappointed them.

In *Out of Africa,* Karen wrote: "Looking back on a sojourn in the African highlands, you are struck by your feeling of having lived for a time up in the air. . . . In the middle of the day the air was alive over the land, like a flame burning; it scintillated, waved and shone like running water. . . . Up in this high air you breathed easily,

75

drawing in a vital assurance and lightness of heart. In the highlands you woke up in the morning and thought: Here I am, where I ought to be."

Beryl woke up one spring morning, three years after her wedding, and knew that living with Jock was not where she wanted to be. But her father and Green Hill Farm were gone. So too were *arap* Maina and Lady Delamere. Beryl mounted Pegasus and rode to Mbogani. Karen was sympathetic to Beryl's situation and took her in. In a letter to her mother in Denmark, Karen wrote that Beryl Purves was staying with her for a time. "She is only twenty, really one of the most beautiful girls I have seen," she wrote, "but she has had such bad luck. She is married to a man she doesn't care for, and he won't agree to a divorce, nor will he give her any allowance, so she is pretty stranded—but full of life and energy, so I expect she will manage. . . ."

While staying at Mbogani, Beryl mingled with the Baroness's acquaintances and house guests. Among them were a wealthy Irish immigrant, Lord John Carberry (called J. C.), and his wife, Maia. Berkeley Cole, who was the brother of Lady Delamere, and his friend, Denys Finch Hatton, were also frequent guests. Finch Hatton, in particular, caught Beryl's eye. He was handsome and rugged, a drifter and a decent who earned his living like Blix, leading wealthy tourists on safari. Between camping excursions, he lived at Mbogani with Karen. He was British and well-educated. He appreciated good wine and good music and literature. Karen and Denys often sat long into the evenings discussing philosophy or Shakespeare. Beryl, who knew nothing of such things, remained on the outer rim of their conversations.

Both J. C. Carberry and Denys Finch Hatton had a fascination with the newest machine to penetrate Africa's wilderness. It was not the Iron Snake, the Model T truck, or the motorcycle, though more roads were being cut through the bush and hills to make way for cars and cycles. The machine that had sparked Carberry's and Finch Hatton's imaginations was the airplane. J. C. was even teaching Maia how to fly. Beryl's curiosity was aroused. One day, with Denys' encouragement, she would exchange her horse with wings for another with wings of metal. One day, also, with J. C.'s support, she would make aviation history. But for the moment, she was still rooted to the earth, a trainer of racehorses.

After a few weeks of refuge at Mbogani, Beryl returned to Jock, but not out of any sense of loyalty and certainly not out of love. Full of self-pity, Jock had cried openly to his friends about Beryl's bad treatment of him. When he drank, his temper quickened and he created rows, in private and in public, accusing her of having affairs with other men. Even though his accusations were probably true, the African *syces* who worked for Jock did not respect him. Neither did Beryl. Jock Purves was no Denys Finch Hatton. But Jock owned the horses, and he held her purse strings. For a while longer, Beryl needed him.

A particularly bad scene that occurred in Nakuru in 1923, however, complicated matters, not only for Beryl and Jock's marriage but also for Lord Delamere's reputation. Clutt had been gone for nearly three years, and Lord Delamere had become a sort of surrogate father to Beryl. She continued to visit him at his ranch at Soysambu, as she had done as a child. She was now also training his horses. On a December night outside a Nakuru hotel, Jock accused Lord Delamere's son Tom of trying to steal Beryl from him. Jock had been drinking, and he pointed an angry finger at Lord Delamere's manager, a man called Boy Long. He, too, had eyes for Beryl, Jock swore. He demanded that Lord Delamere put a stop to the ugly situation happening in his stable or he would stop it himself. He threatened to shoot Long.

What happened next is not clear. Lord Delamere might have tried to reason with Jock. Perhaps he spoke in his son's or even in Beryl's defense. Or he might have become angry, for he was known to have a violent temper when aroused. Whatever Lord Delamere might have said or done, Jock attacked him. By the time friends had pulled Jock away, Lord Delamere lay seriously wounded on the hotel steps. His jaw was broken as were several bones in his arm.

Karen Blixen wrote about the ugly scene at Nakuru in a letter to her mother: "[Lord Delamere] will be in bed at least six months. For the sake of his son and Beryl, Delamere does not want the cause of his injuries made public, but everybody knows about it."

Everyone did know. And everyone disapproved, but not of Jock's behavior—of Beryl's. Lord Delamere was an important man politically among the European settlers in Kenya Colony. That he had been so seriously hurt in a brawl over Beryl scandalized the local society. It did not matter if Delamere had tried to defend her honor or if, even from his sickbed, he wanted to protect her. Nor did it matter if Jock drank or was abusive to his beautiful and much younger wife. What mattered was Beryl's bad behavior, leaving Jock for days and sometimes weeks at a time or blatantly flirting with other men in front of him. Even Karen, who at one time had been sympathetic to Beryl's situation, called the fight at Nakuru "an awful mess" and thought it better if Beryl stayed away from the races for a time.

In *West with the Night,* Beryl chose the memories from her life that she wanted to share with her readers. She devoted pages to her relationships with *arap* Maina, Kibii, her father, even Buller and the horses. But she chose not to write about Jock. In the book, he simply doesn't exist. A particularly moving chapter, however, describes the night she left Njoro for good.

It was Christmastime and cold, though not snowy. Buller was dead. She had long ago buried him herself at a spot overlooking the valley, piling a pyramid of rocks on his grave so that no hyena or any other scavenger could get to him. Her father was gone, along with most of the horses. Even her old friend Kibii had moved on. Beryl no longer had a reason to stay. She saddled Pegasus, slipped the bit into his mouth, and led him out of the stable. To the north was Molo, the place where her father had advised her to go. To the north was where she now nudged Pegasus.

"We left before dawn," she wrote, "so that when the hills again took shape Njoro was gone, disappeared with the last impotent scowl of night."

What she did not write was whether Jock knew she was leaving or if, by slipping away under cloak of night, she was escaping from him. The words "impotent scowl" might have been her own secret reference to the man who had refused to give her a divorce. After years of enduring him, Beryl solved the problem in the same way she had solved so many of her problems as a child—by running away. This time, however, she was not running home to her father. She could not. Nor was she running to Lord Delamere or Baroness Blixen. After the embarrassing ruckus at Nakuru, Beryl was smart to avoid knocking on those doors again too soon.

No, her father had been right. Molo was the place. Perhaps there she could start a new life.

She rode all night. Traveling alone through the Mau Forest—day or night—is not without danger. Beryl relied on surefooted Pegasus to carry her through the hills. As one life disappeared with the night behind her, another began to take shape with the dawning of the new day before her. "The new sun falls . . . in a jumble of golden bars," Beryl wrote. As she and Pegasus pressed on through the forest, antelope and giant bush-pigs fled from their path. Overhead were laughing monkeys and all around were vividly colored butterflies. As she rode farther north, the air remained chilled even with the morning sun, and Beryl slipped into a buckskin jacket. The land now looked more like the highlands of Scotland than of Africa. Thick ferns stitched icy streams. Heather covered the hills. At a stream, Beryl stopped to let Pegasus rest and drink. His ears, tilted back, and his eyes, wide and searching, told her he was uneasy. This higher, colder place was unfamiliar.

"He scuffs the ground and lowers his head to nudge

my shoulder, coaxing me gently, suggesting, I suspect, that we go back the way we came."

But the sun moves in only one direction across the sky. Time cannot be reversed. Memories can be selected and either saved or discarded, but events cannot be relived. After resting a while, Beryl mounted Pegasus and nudged him forward again. In one saddle bag were oats for him to eat. In the other were Beryl's pajamas, a fresh shirt, slacks, and a toothbrush. They were all she owned in the world.

nine

Wise Child

B eryl was good at putting on a confident face, at swallowing her fear and enduring pain. Like her father, she did not boast about her winnings or whine about her losses. But underneath her skin of confidence was self-doubt and the ever-present loneliness.

"If only there were someone to trust—someone I know," Beryl wrote. "But, of course, there isn't. Not now. This is not Njoro in past days when I was a child and had a friend or two. This is Molo in the new days with new friends still in the making. Where are the old? Where are they ever?"

Beryl was counting on the unwritten law of African hospitality when she called upon Mrs. Carsdale-Luck in Molo. In East Africa, one did not turn away a guest, whether friend or enemy. It was too rugged, too lonely a country to risk not giving (and therefore receiving in return) comfort or assistance when it was needed. But Beryl needed more than just a place to live for a few days or weeks. She needed a job. To get that, Beryl was counting on something more than just hospitality.

Mrs. Carsdale-Luck and her husband owned one of Camciscan's sons, a promising yearling named Wrack. Beryl struck a deal. She had no money. But she had a knowledge of horses, and not just any horses. She had helped to train the high-strung stallion that had sired Wrack. In exchange for loaned stable space and a place to live, she would train their horses. Just as Karen Blixen had once given Beryl refuge, Mrs. Carsdale-Luck now offered Beryl a thatched hut in which to live. The hut was similar to the Beryl's rondavel at Green Hill Farm. Giving Beryl a place to start her life over was one thing. Trusting such a young woman with racehorses was another thing altogether. Even though Beryl had won races in the past, she had been financed by Jock and his partners. And she had had the support of Lord Delamere. Molo was a new place with a new stable of horses. But without Clutt and without Jock's financial support, could she still succeed?

Beryl must have slipped on her skin of confidence at that point and said that she most certainly could succeed, for the Carsdale-Lucks agreed to the arrangement.

In her new life, Beryl would have to prove her worth all over again. She began at once, rising each day at five o'clock. Wrack was a chestnut colt, headstrong like his father had been. Wrack could run but he needed discipline. Welsh Guard was another of Camiscan's sons, but not as promising as Wrack. The other horses in her stable were dull. But each on its turn, she examined, groomed, rode, trained, and evaluated. Which one had tender legs? Which one would pull hard under the jockey's whip? At sunset, she returned to her hut, furnished simply with an iron bed, a table and chair, and a hurricane lamp. Now it was she, not Clutt, who sat in the lamp's dull light and scribbled notes and added and subtracted numbers. In six weeks was the Race Meeting at Nairobi. Beryl desperately needed a winner. Even in the lamp's dull light, it was clear to her. She needed more time. She could not do it alone.

One night, the sound of barefeet approaching the hut alerted her. She set down her pen. Outside the door stood a tall man, an African. He wore a red *shuka*, or blanket, knotted over one shoulder. From a chain around his neck hung a lion's claw. Around his ankles were the furry black and white tails of Colobus monkeys. Beryl did not know him or why he had come. Still, she welcomed him inside.

As the man stepped through the door and into the feeble light, Beryl realized all at once that she was no longer alone. He was from her past, only he was no longer called Kibii. He was *murani* now, a warrior. As a man, he had taken a new name, *arap* Ruta.

Beryl might have fled Njoro during the night and in secret, but she had not completely disappeared. People knew where she had gone. When *arap* Ruta returned to Njoro and discovered that Green Hill Farm was no more, he set out to find Beryl. Their reunion at Molo was joyful. Each had found a lost friend. But it was sad as well for their relationship had changed. Although *arap* Ruta offered to work for her, neither he nor Beryl were the children they had once been. Then they had walked together as equals. But now *arap* Ruta walked a few steps behind her, for even though he was *murani,* she was still the *memsahib.* It was not her choice that he should shadow her. It was just the way things were.

Arap Ruta left Molo but returned again soon after with

his wife. Clutt had taught him much about horses. Now, with his help, Beryl looked toward the Race Meeting in Nairobi with new hope.

Arap Ruta had found her at Molo. At Molo, Beryl found Tom Campbell Black. She was riding Pegasus across a treeless plain. Tom was riding in an automobile—or had been. It had broken down, and he was using a pair of pliers on the engine. Once again the unwritten law of African hospitality came into play. Without hesitation, Beryl dismounted and offered to help. She knew far more about horses than car engines, and so she mostly waited in the sun while he worked at trying to get the engine to start again.

They talked, about cars at first. Beryl thought the car "an intrusion . . . a foolish toy" dropped in the middle of an African plain. Tom's answer, as Beryl recorded it in *West with the Night,* was prophetic. "You can't stop things, you know," he had said. "One day when roads are built, this whole country will be rumbling with trains and cars—and we'll all get used to it."

It was happening already. Since the war, more ex-soldiers—men like Tom—had settled in Kenya Colony. Their farmhouses were made of stone, not mud and wattle. Their gardens were hemmed by hedges in straight rows. Nairobi, not even a quarter of a century old, was already a modern city with parking meters instead of hitching posts. And from its center, newly built roads, like finger traces in the sand, were beginning to reach into the highlands and as far north as Molo. The roads were bad, deeply rutted or gummed with mud when it rained, but they were roads nevertheless in places where roads had never been before.

They talked some more. Tom said he had flown during the war, and his dream was to buy an airplane of his own. First Denys Finch Hatton and J. C. Carberry, now Tom Black—what was it about airplanes that appealed so to men? Tom had an explanation for that, as well.

"When you fly," the young man said, "you get a feeling of possession that you couldn't have if you owned all of Africa. You feel that everything you see belongs to you —all the pieces are put together, and the whole is yours."

It sounded like freedom to Beryl, like *Lakweit* escaping through the tunnels of tall wet grass. Theirs was a chance meeting in a remote place. But change and chance go hand-in-hand. One triggers the other. Tom had planted a seed in her imagination. As she mounted Pegasus and waved good-bye, Beryl had no way of knowing that the seed would one day take root and change her life completely.

Wrack did not disappoint. In July 1925, Beryl and *arap* Ruta took him to Nairobi where the son of Camciscan took a very respectable second place. His next time at the gate, he took first. Beryl was back in the winner's circle.

She did not own the winning horses, of course. The prize money from the races went to the owners, not her. And yet, success was like a magnet. Beryl's winning season drew new owners and their horses to her stables. Soon, she outgrew the loaned stalls in Molo. Money was still tight, but the time had come for her to return to the mainstream. When she moved her operation to the Nakuru Race Course in 1926, she did not own much more than the contents of the two saddle bags with which she had fled Njoro more than a year earlier. But she had the confidence of a growing number of horse owners. And she had *arap* Ruta. He and his wife moved with her.

She could not afford a house at Nakuru any more than she could have at Molo, but that did not bother her. She pitched a tent near the stables. Beyond was a lake that was home to flocks of pink flamingoes. Beryl called it "the lake of pink and scarlet wings" for only the long-legged flamingoes could tolerate the high amounts of sodium carbonate in the lake's waters. Their albino eyes looked as if they had been singed by the soda. At sunset the lake turned golden. Beryl was once again where she wanted to be, doing what she loved best—training horses.

At sunrise, she could be seen riding Wise Child across the mud flats of the lake shore. The filly had been born in Clutt's stables at Njoro. Beryl had midwifed the birth, as she had with Pegasus. But the filly's early life had not been easy. Her first owner had pushed her too hard and damaged the tendons in her legs. Her present owner returned the horse to Beryl to see what could be done to salvage his thoroughbred investment. Beryl believed that the morning exercise across the soft lake shore could stretch and strengthen Wise Child's weak legs. To run her on any surface that was harder than soft mud would destroy her legs for good. With time, work, and patience, Wise Child could become a contender for the Saint Leger Cup in Nairobi.

As a child, Beryl had lived in a world of absolutes. It was the same on the racetrack as it was in the bush. Either a horse won the race or it lost. Placing second or third meant nothing. Once the race had been run, it could not be run again. After twelve weeks of training, Beryl decided that Wise Child was ready to run, but she doubted that she could win. But Beryl had no choice. Wrack's owner had taken him away from her. Wise Child was her best bet for the Saint Leger.

Beryl's cool exterior often camouflaged a nervousness she felt in the last hours before a race. The Saint Leger, in particular, was a very important one. It was not only a grand social event in Kenya Colony, with settlers arriving in Nairobi from all points and attending private dances and parties; it was also about money. A great deal of money, in fact, would be bet and lost in a very short time. She and *arap* Ruta worked silently together in the stall, preparing Wise Child for the post. They examined her legs for swelling and fever. They lifted each hoof and studied it. The racing bridle, the harness, the number cloth, the saddle—each in its turn was fitted on the filly. Beryl had learned to think like a horse, and, in the stall before the race, she had a silent conversation with Wise Child. The way the horse turned her head toward Beryl was like a question: How much longer? The way she nuzzled against Beryl was like a promise: I will do what you ask.

The bell sounded, calling the ten horses to the post. Beryl passed Wise Child into the hands of her jockey, Sonny Bumpus. Training is one important element to a race. A well-trained horse will fly like the wind. Strategy is another essential element. With Wise Child's weak legs, she needed time to warm up. Once she reached the far stretch, Sonny could push her, but not until then and not if her legs were unsteady.

Remembering that important race, Beryl said she tried to appear "casual" but her hands were shaking. Winning was important, of course. Beryl was not foolish. To win was why she had entered this man's game. Winning the Saint Leger could seal her future as a horse trainer in Kenya. But Beryl's worry beyond the win was that Wise Child's legs might not hold up. A friend standing beside her at the rail told her she was trembling. She only smiled.

Once the bell sounded and the horses exploded from the gate, Beryl's trembling ceased. Like the sun crossing the sky, there could be no turning back now. Wise Child would win or she would lose. Her legs would carry her or she would stumble. Beryl could do nothing more now except watch.

The race was a thriller. Sonny held Wise Child back, as was Beryl's strategy. On the far stretch, he her let run. Wise Child took the lead, surprising the crowd of spectators who knew her history and had not expected her to perform. Then, just when it seemed victory was hers, her legs gave out. She stumbled. The crowd—and Beryl, too—gasped. Somehow, Wise Child recovered and thundered across the finish line, still in the lead. Beryl said she had run not on three legs, but on her heart.

Wise Child had won the Saint Leger Classic, and in doing so, had set a new track record. The win was Beryl's greatest achievement thus far, though her name as trainer was omitted from the newspaper. The omission of the name of the only woman trainer in the field might have simply been an accident. Or it could have been a sexist sting, reminding Beryl that she was playing a man's game. Whatever the reason, she seemed not to care. Publicity did not win races. The horse owners knew who had trained the winner. Had he been there to see Beryl's victory, Clutt would have been proud.

ten

Pioneer of the Skies

Once she had been called *Lakweit*. Now the Africans had a new name for her: *Memsahib wa Farusi*, or Lady of the Horses.

Beryl had redeemed her father's reputation. She had redeemed her own as well. Her continued wins on the racetrack throughout 1926 made her a sort of local celebrity in Nairobi and Nakuru. She was invited to house parties and dinner engagements at the homes of the wealthy emigrants. Karen Blixen wrote to her mother: "I saw Beryl recently, she seemed very happy, working hard training racehorses . . ." The Baroness, the J. C. Carberrys, and others sought Beryl out not as Jock Purves's wife, for Beryl was now legally divorced from him, but as a woman who was intriguing and successful in her own right. She did not drink much at these parties where champagne was often served by the case. Instead, she preferred to sit quietly in a corner and talk or simply observe the other guests, most of whom—unlike her—did not have to work for a living.

One such guest was Mansfield Markham. The

Markham family had made its fortune in the steel industry in England. Mansfield and his older brother Charles were visiting Kenya in order to purchase property in the Kenyan highlands as a winter home for their mother, Lady Markham. Mixing business with pleasure, the two brothers also intended to go on safari before returning to England. Opera and architecture, literature and botany were the stuff that mattered most to Mansfield. Beryl knew nothing about the arts and sciences, and her social graces were not very polished, either. Nevertheless, Mansfield Markham saw in Beryl something wild and beautiful he wanted to possess. He canceled his plans to go on safari.

They were worlds apart. Everyone who knew them both agreed on that. He was England. She was Africa. He was cultured and sophisticated. She was daring and fearless. He was intelligent, not very athletic, and had been ill with tuberculosis as a child. She was intelligent, as strong as a man, and still bore the childhood scars of a lion's claws and horses' teeth. He was an aristocrat. She was *Memsahib wa Farasi*. Still, within weeks of meeting each other, they became engaged.

Karen Blixen, who knew both Mansfield and Beryl, probably looked upon their sudden engagement with doubt that their marriage could last. After all, Mansfield was a respectable. But Beryl was a decent. If Mansfield wanted to possess her and change her, he was bound to be disappointed, for a decent belongs to no one but God.

Ada was no longer around to plan the wedding details. And so it was Mansfield who selected Beryl's dress of crepe de chine. He also persuaded her to cut her long blonde hair into a short shingle, a popular hairstyle of the late 1920s. Clutt was gone. And so Lord Delamere stood in his place and gave the bride away. Unlike Beryl's last marriage, the Mansfield wedding party was warmly welcomed at the Muthaiga Country Club.

Three rows of people are seated around Beryl in her wedding portrait. The Baroness Von Blixen sits with her head cocked to one side. Lord Delamere's hair is white with age. A surprising family member is also in attendance—Clara Clutterbuck. Beryl's mother had returned to Africa a few years earlier soon after the death of her second husband, and she brought her two young boys with her. Although Beryl rarely spoke to her mother and avoided her whenever she could, she rather liked the boys and called them her "brothers." They, too, are in the picture, seated on the ground at Beryl's feet. Everyone looks forward into the eye of the camera. Only Beryl, with her short, straight hair, glances away.

A newspaper article dated September 3, 1927, announced the Markham marriage, describing it as "quiet but fashionable." The married couple dashed from Saint Andrew's Church under a bridge of crossed racing whips and through a sudden storm of confetti. After the wedding, the couple departed Kenya for a honeymoon in Europe. *Arap* Ruta went with them as Beryl's personal servant.

It seemed as if another new life was about to begin for Beryl. In fact, it was, but Mansfield Markham would not be a part of it for very long. Like the string of people who had preceded him—Clara Clutterbuck, Ada Orchardson, Miss Le May, Jock Purves—Markham soon would be left behind.

As Mrs. Markham, Beryl could now afford to buy excellent horses for her stables. She need not concern herself any longer with cast-offs, the dull and the lame horses that doubtful owners had brought to her as a last resort at saving their investment. Markham's wealth also made it possible for Clutt to return from Peru, which he did with Ada in 1928. The roles of father and daughter were reversed—Clutt worked for Beryl now, managing the Markhams' growing stable of horses.

Beryl described this time in her life as one of contentment. But she described the contentment as "a slumber." She was sleeping, not living, for challenge was what kept her alive. Then a series of events occurred that shook her awake.

In 1928, she became pregnant, a predicament that appalled her. Beryl had grown up without a mother's care. Just as she understood little about the duties expected of a wife when she married Jock Purves, she knew nothing now about taking care of a baby. She did not welcome motherhood. When the time neared for her to deliver her baby, she traveled to England. A boy was born there on February 27, 1929, with a deformity that required a number of operations. This further horrified Beryl, who in her African world of absolutes could not accept a child that was not healthy. As her biographer Errol Trezbinski explains, "In Kipsigis culture, midwives decided the fate of any child suffering abnormality. The infant would be placed on the ground outside the hut. If the baby was meant to live, it would survive the pounding hooves as the herdsmen drove their stock out to graze, *shaurie ya mungu*—God's will—and accordingly was nurtured. If it perished, that was that."

Just as Clara had abandoned her daughter, Beryl seemed more than willing to relinquish her son to her mother-in-law, Lady Markham's, care and upbringing. Her brother Richard had not survived for long in the African highlands. Beryl had no reason to believe her sickly son would either. At least with Lady Markham, Gervase—as he was named—would have a chance at survival. Perhaps to Beryl, leaving him in England must have been no different than placing the infant on the ground outside the hut and letting God decide his fate. Gervase did survive, but he grew up not knowing his mother.

The second event that occurred was the death of Denys Finch Hatton. Denys had become more than just a friend to Beryl. Since the days when she had stayed with Karen Blixen at Mbogani, Beryl had been powerfully attracted to this great white hunter. It mattered little to her that Karen was also in love with him. Nor did it matter that Beryl was married to Mansfield. She had continued to pursue Finch Hatton.

Then one day Denys died in a flying accident. He had flown his Gypsy Moth airplane on an excursion to Voi, near the coast, to test a theory. As a safari scout, his job was to lead his clients to the four big game animals they wished to kill: water buffalo, lions, leopards, and tuskers. Tuskers, or elephants, were a challenge. Locating a herd often took days or even weeks. Denys believed that scouting elephants by air could save a great deal of time and effort. Karen Blixen asked to go with him on the overnight flight to Voi, but he turned her down. A few days later he was with Beryl at the Muthiaga Country

Club, and he invited her to go with him instead. Without hesitating, she accepted. However, Tom Black changed her mind. He was teaching her how to fly. He was a strict teacher, as Clutt had been, and he argued that Beryl could not miss a lesson. Beryl canceled her plans. Had she not, she most surely would have died in the fiery plane crash with Denys.

Denys' sudden death was a terrible shock to Karen Blixen. She mourned him as a husband. Beryl had a husband, but she, too, grieved. Beryl did not love Mansfield, but she had been in love with Denys. Beryl's friends in Kenya, the same friends who had attended Karen Blixen's parties and who dined and danced at the Muthiaga Country Club, believed this. They often saw Beryl and Denys together. Beryl never admitted being in love, however. She was too private a person to share her feelings with others. As always, she cloaked her emotions in words that were carefully chosen. "Denys' death left some lives without design," she wrote in her memoir, "but they were rebuilt again, as lives and stones are, into other patterns." She could have been referring to Karen Blixen. Denys' death had surely left a hole in Karen's life. But since Beryl never mentions the Baroness in *West with the Night,* it is more likely that Beryl was describing her own loss.

The third event that woke Beryl from her slumber of contentment was the drumming sound of airplane engines in the African sky. Tom Black brought the sound home to her. She had flown many times with Denys, but always in the passenger seat in front of the pilot. But with Tom Black as her instructor, she sat in the cockpit and managed the controls. The power of flying an airplane and the freedom of being able to escape the land and soar over it thrilled her.

"You can't stop things, you know," Tom had told her that day long ago at Molo when she happened upon him and his broken car. He was right. Africa was changing and Beryl was changing with it.

"Ruta," she said one morning in the stables, "I think I am going to leave all this and learn to fly." Learning to fly meant earning her pilot's B license and being able to carry mail and passengers, and so earn a living.

He looked out the stable door at what was then their home—fenced paddocks and satin-backed thoroughbreds gleamed in the sun. He did not question Beryl's decision. "He said, If it is to be that we must fly, Memsahib, then we will fly. At what hour of the morning do we begin?"

And so it was that Tom Black provided the stones for Beryl to recreate her life once again. She gave up the acres of fenced paddocks and the satin-backed thoroughbreds. Or rather, she relinquished the care of them, as she had her son, to another—her father. Clutt did not approve of flying. He shook his head, not understanding Beryl's fascination with speed, with getting to one place or another in a matter of hours or days rather than weeks or months. But flying meant more to Beryl than just getting someplace quickly. With Tom as her mentor, she had learned that "a man can be master of a craft" and that "a craft can be master of an element." That kind of power lured Beryl like a moth to light.

Had she been younger, Beryl might have bent under her father's opinion. But she had witnessed his failure. He had lost Green Hill Farm. Since then, she had tasted success on her own without him. Her determination now was to taste success again as a commercial pilot.

She left Mansfield. The luxuries he could provide for her as his wife simply did not satisfy her need to take risks and feel alive. Too much slumber had dulled her senses. She moved to Nairobi and rented a small cottage. Her one loyal friend, *arap* Ruta, went with her and lived in nearby quarters. She was twenty-nine years old, very near the same age that Karen Dinesen had been when she left Denmark to begin her life's great adventure in East Africa. Now it was Beryl's turn. She was about to begin the most challenging and most eventful years of her life. She set her sights on the horizon and a machine that was heavier than air, and she took flight.

Horseracing had been a man's game that Beryl had boldly entered and won. Flying, however, was a new field for both men and women. In the United States, in France, in England, women were donning aviator suits and goggles and taking to the skies, performing loop-the-loops and setting long-distance endurance records. In Kenya, Beryl climbed into the cockpit of a Gypsy Moth and entered the world of aviation.

One thing replaces another in time. Once *arap* Maina had instructed her. "Bend down and look so that you may learn," he had commanded. "See how this leaf is crushed. Feel the wetness of this dung."

Now Tom Black was her teacher. "Trust this," said Tom, referring to the compass, "but nothing else."

"Instruments can go wrong," he said. "If you can't fly

without looking at your airspeed and your altimeter and your bank-and-turn indicator—well, then you can't fly. You're like somebody who only knows what he thinks after reading his newspaper. But don't mistrust the compass—your judgment will never be more accurate than that needle."

When the subject interested her, Beryl was an excellent pupil. She listened and she learned.

Flying in Africa in the early 1930s was hazardous. Nairobi had a small, fledgling airport with a grass landing strip called the Wilson Airdrome. But where Beryl wanted to go—needed to go if she was to become a commercial pilot—runways often did not exist. The pilot, or those working with the pilot, had to hack out of the bush or forest a long enough strip to accommodate take-offs and landings. Once up, terrific down drafts caused by the heat or sudden storms sweeping in from the coast could pound a plane into the side of a mountain.

Landing was no easy feat, either. A wild pig hole could cripple a horse should the animal be unfortunate enough to stumble into it during a gallop. A pig hole could also snag the wheel of an airplane, and the resulting slam could rip off a wing or crack a propeller. Herds of zebra or Thompson's gazelles or any wild animal that wandered onto the make-shift landing strip could cause a crash. At night, a few oil hurricane lamps, a bonfire, or car headlights served as landing lights for the pilot. There were no control towers or radar guidance systems. Such were the conditions for pilots in Kenya in the 1930s. Beryl was a pioneer of the African skies in much the same way that Clutt had been a pioneer of the land in 1904.

Hour by hour, Beryl gained flying experience. As a child she had thought the cedars of the Mau Forest so tall "their branches brushed the sky." Now, she was flying over them. Instead of jotting down the names and statistics of horses in a black book each night, she now recorded her flying hours and routes in a log book. Just as a horse needs to be groomed and examined for swollen tendons and cracked hooves, so too an airplane needs to be maintained. Beryl learned how to take apart an engine, how to replace spark plugs, and how to clean jets. Just as a horserace relies on strategy to beat the odds on a race-track, a flight requires a map. Beryl learned how to read maps and to trust their lines and blots. Without a map, she said, a pilot was blind.

After eighteen months and nearly one thousand flying hours to her credit, Beryl applied for her B license under British regulations. The board granted her request. Beryl had become a commercial pilot.

One thing replaces another in time.

eleven

Safari Nights

Tom worried about her. He thought she was pushing herself too hard, living on her nerves, as he put it. For months, Beryl had been piloting mail and passengers across Africa, logging hundreds of hours of flying time. She also flew rescue missions, and more than once her airplane had served as an ambulance in the bush. But that was not what alarmed Tom. What worried him was Beryl's new plan to work for Karen Blixen's husband, Blix.

Karen Blixen had returned to Denmark in 1931 after her coffee plantation went bankrupt. All her property and furnishings had been sold at auction just as Clutt's property in Njoro had been sold. Her lover, Denys Finch Hatton, was dead. She had little reason to stay in Kenya. Tom had also left Africa. He had accepted a job as a private pilot for a wealthy British aristocrat. But Blix had stayed. As Bwana Blix, he was one of the best white hunters in Africa and was particularly in demand since Denys' death. Now Blix was urging Beryl to fulfill Denys' dream of scouting elephant by air.

". . . If you had one grain of sense," Tom wrote to Beryl from London, "you wouldn't make a regular habit of flying for elephant in elephant country. . . . It's sheer madness and bloodily dangerous."

But on Beryl's table was a telegram that she had received the same day. "Be at Makindu tomorrow seven a.m. . . . Makula report herd elephant with big bull . . . Blix."

She trusted Tom's opinion. In teaching her how to fly, he had not neglected to include all the things that could go wrong for a pilot in the bush—down drafts, sudden storms, low fuel, and no place to land. Once down, a pilot had to cope with malaria, tsetse fly, blackwater fever, and—Beryl's worse nightmare—Siafu. When she flew, Beryl always carried a vial of morphine in a pocket of her aviator's jumpsuit, just in case. She called it her "doctor's bottled sleep."

But Blix was offering her three times the money she was currently earning as a commercial pilot, and something else equally valuable—adventure. Beryl simply could not resist. "Don't worry," she wrote back to Tom. "I know you're absolutely right, and I intend to quit it as soon as I can. . ."

But, she added, she was flying down to Makindu in the morning just the same. She signed her letter, "Tail winds and happy landings."

Safari was big business. "Have the time of your life and thrills galore," advertised a poster from the 1920s. "Photograph and shoot big game in the world's best game country, Kenya."

And the hunters came from all over the world. In the

early days, when Beryl was still *Lakweit* and running through the bush behind *arap* Maina, the safari hunters traveled upcountry first by train, then by ox-drawn carts and wagons, then on foot, followed by a string of hired porters. Safari supplies to last weeks or months were carefully inventoried. In addition to camp tents, chairs, and tables, crates of canned peaches, baked beans, and tomatoes were also packed, as were pints of whiskey and cases of champagne. Whiskey doubled as a medicine when needed.

In the 1930s, however, cars and trucks—and airplanes—were used to reach the game. Additional supplies and even mail could be flown to a remote safari camp. In fact, Blix's telegram had requested that Beryl bring fifty more rounds of ammunition and six additional bottles of gin. In the early days, the Bwana leading the safari might spend weeks, even months tracking a single bull tusker. In the 1930s, Denys' theory, which Beryl now put into action, was that a pilot could spot the tuskers from the air and report their location by radio to the camp. The rules of the game had changed.

"The game is both the hunt and the hunted, the sport and the trophy," wrote Peter Beard in his book about the destruction the white settlement in BEA had inflicted on the land and the wildlife. "The game is killing the game."

Blix was excellent at the game. And in the 1930s, the forested area of Tsavo beyond Nairobi was still "so swollen with game it could have been a hunter's dream of prehistory," said Beard. Blix led his monied clients back in time, hundreds of miles into the interior of Africa. He blazed new trails, using bush knives to clear the thick foliage. He felled trees and dug up stumps to build a level landing strip for Beryl's light airplane. When one area had been hunted, he moved to another. What made him so good, besides the fact that he was an excellent shot, was that he did not give up until his clients bagged the trophies for which they had come to this hunter's paradise.

That was where Beryl was most helpful to Blix. Sometimes Blix flew with her to scout for the elephants. Most times, though, *arap* Ruta swung the propeller to engage the engines, and Beryl took off from the safari camp at dawn, alone. She flew low without a radio, searching the shapes and shadows on the land. When she spotted what she thought was worthwhile game for the killing, she scribbled a note on a pad of paper which she kept tied to her right leg for that very purpose, she then slipped it into a message bag with a tail of blue and gold ribbons and hurled it out of the plane. The colored ribbons made spotting the message easier for Blix.

Why did she do it? She loved the land. She admired and respected the clean efficiency of life in the wild. The sight of ten thousand wildebeests migrating with the rains, unbranded by humans, thrilled her. How then could she become a party to Kenya's destruction by leading hunters to the prey?

A letter written by Karen Blixen provides a clue. When she had lived in Africa, Karen had found safari an exhilarating experience. Safari life, she wrote, "makes you forget all your sorrows and feel the whole time as if you had drunk half a bottle of champagne—bubbling over with heartfelt gratitude for being alive."

Given her seemingly insatiable thirst for adventure

and risk, Beryl must have felt the same, even though her safari duty was hundreds of feet above the earth and she herself did not shoot the animals. Then there was the matter of money, of course. Beryl had separated from Mansfield and needed to find the coins to fill her purse. Beyond those reasons, however, safari was—and had been for as long as Beryl had lived in Africa—a way of life.

There were important differences between the African way of hunting and the white safaris. Nandi and Masai hunted lions and wart hogs with spears and killed only what they needed or required to fulfill tribal rituals. The wealthy tourists, on the other hand, hunted with heavy rifles and killed for no other reason than to pose for a photograph with one foot on the hide of a dead beast or to bring home the severed head or horns or tusks to mount on a wall.

A lion can run forty miles per hour, and the Nandi and Masai hunters pursued lions on foot. They were able to, because they had trained to run long distances. They circled an animal, then closed the circle, and lunged with their spears. The bravest hunter among them was often awarded the lion's tail for a trophy. The wealthy white hunters, on the other hand, baited their prey by first killing a zebra or a wildebeest, then dragging it to a place where lions had been spotted. They returned to their safari camp in the afternoon for tea. At dawn the next morning, the hunters returned to the kill and shot the lion that had happened upon the free meal. If the hunter's shot missed, the Bwana immediately raised his rifle and expertly finished the job.

Both hunting rituals—black and white—existed in

Kenya in the 1930s. No doubt Beryl thought the African way of life more admirable. It certainly was more courageous and skillful. But the white safaris were definitely profitable.

"It is absurd for a man to kill an elephant," Beryl wrote in *West with the Night*. "It is not brutal, it is not heroic, and certainly it is not easy; it is just one of those preposterous things that men do like putting a dam across a great river." She added, "I suppose there is nothing more tragic about the death of an elephant than there is about the death of a Hereford steer—certainly not in the eyes of the steer. The only difference is that the steer has neither the ability nor the chance to outwit the gentleman . . ."

As a child, watching Clutt bait the leopard with a tethered goat, take aim, and never miss, Beryl had learned not to be sentimental about killing in Africa. Nor was she sentimental as the first bush pilot to scout elephant by the air. As she had said once before in Molo, a job was a job. And if it came with adventure, well then, all the better.

The shadow of her Avian plane grumbled as it raced over the bush. By now the elephants were wise to the sound. On the first encounter with the Avian that flew noisily above them, they took cover in dense thicket. Beryl lost sight of them, that is she could no longer distinguish them from boulders. On her second encounter, usually on the following day, the elephants adopted a different strategy that amazed Beryl. The females, she said, "grouped themselves" around the bulls so that from the cockpit

Beryl could not be sure if a worthwhile tusker was among them. Beryl concluded that the females knew the Avian was hunting the bulls for their 100-pound ivory and that their own small tusks were of little value in comparison. At those times, Beryl was often forced to push in her control stick and dive low over the massive gray huddle in an attempt to lodge the elephants apart. Tom was right. It was bloodily dangerous. If the Avian could not gain altitude again quick enough . . . if she were forced to land on sansevieria that could spear the belly of her plane . . .

Well, such were the risks of the job. She knew what she was getting into when she had accepted Blix's offer.

Beryl kept her eye on the sun. At the equator once the sun sank below the horizon, violet darkness came quickly and posed new risks for a pilot. As shadows began to stretch across the ground, she banked her Avian and returned to the safari camp. She found its location in the thick foliage by first spotting Blix's smoke signals. Then, after circling two or three times to be certain that no wildlife or ant hills could cause her to crash, she landed on the "miserly" runway Blix, or rather his porters, had built for her. Later, seated in front of a campfire, Beryl listened to the laughter of the hyenas in the jungle around her. Safari nights were also nights of leopards, nights of lions. The cackling and soft growling were familiar sounds to her and not particularly frightening. They reminded her of Njoro and what she had left behind.

At times, Beryl must have regretted the decisions she had made—leaving Njoro, leaving her horses, leaving her father, for she wrote in *West with the Night,* "It is no good telling yourself that one day you will wish you had never made that change. . . . Every tomorrow ought not to resemble every yesterday." It was the moral of the story about the egret which Ruta had told her long, long ago when they were both children. They were no longer children. And Africa was no longer a pioneer's country.

Safari nights—and many of the days, as well—were lonely, even when *arap* Ruta accompanied her on the excursions. One night in front of a campfire, Blix wondered if she had dozed off, she was so quiet, so still. "I spend so much time alone that silence has become a habit," Beryl answered.

On those wistful nights, Beryl thought of Tom and of London. She had promised him that she would quit scouting elephants when she could afford it. She intended to keep her promise. But, when one safari ended, Blix would book another, and off she'd go again.

The 1920s and 1930s were the Golden Age of flying. In other parts of the world, aviators—male and female—were setting flying records. In 1927, Charles Lindbergh had flown solo across the Atlantic Ocean, New York to Paris with the wind behind him. The three thousand mile crossing in a single engine monoplane had taken thirty-three and one-half hours. After he had landed, the world hailed him a hero. But he was not the only one. In 1932, Amelia Earhart became the first woman to fly solo across the Atlantic. Even Tom Black had distinguished himself in 1934 by winning an air race from London to Melbourne, Australia. He and his copilot had flown the distance in just under three days. Such nonstop flights and air races were not frivolous feats intended to make headlines. Airplane manufacturers often sponsored the events in order to learn more about airplane design and endurance.

It is possible that on those safari nights while staring into the campfire and thinking of Tom and of London and of how quite possibly she was doomed to be a lonely drifter all her life, Beryl had begun to dream of setting her own flying record. She was as much a professional pilot as Charles Lindbergh or Amelia Earhart. She would have liked to have been Tom's copilot during that race from England to Australia. Together, they could have made a dynamic flying team. But Tom had not asked her. Earlier in the year, he had married a British actress named Florence Desmond. Beryl had cabled him that she was "heartbroken" by the news. But that was all she said. Tom had not written back to explain why he had chosen another pilot over her. Nor did he apologize for falling in love and marrying another woman.

The same acquaintances who believed that Beryl had fallen in love with Denys Finch Hatton also believed she was stung by Tom's marriage to Florence Desmond. Each time she found a man who could measure up to her father, she somehow lost him.

"A life has to move or it stagnates," Beryl consoled herself. At least, it was what she believed about her own life. Restlessness and curiosity had begun to bubble inside her once more, and with it, the need to prove herself all over again. Perhaps she felt she needed to prove herself to Tom. Whatever the reason, in 1934, Beryl began to consider leaving Africa. In the meantime, until she could figure things out, she continued to fly elephants for Blix.

In 1934, a serious bout of malaria grounded her for months. Her illness could have been the break-away point from flying elephants. But, once recovered, she returned to safari work. Then one day in October, while sitting in a bar with some friends, J. C. Carberry challenged Beryl to attempt flying the Atlantic the wrong way—against the wind, west to east. Two years earlier, another daredevil aviator named Jim Mollison had attempted the westward flight, departing Ireland for New York. He had landed in New Brunswick, Canada, short of his destination. The newspapers had jumped on the story, declaring Mollison's flight a great success and speculating that air transportation between London and New York City would soon become a reality. As of 1934, Amelia Earhart was the only woman to have flown the Atlantic solo and no one—man nor woman—had flown solo from England to New York.

J. C. had a reputation for egging people on. He had once dared his daughter to swim across Mombasa Bay, reminding her of the sharks. Now he teased Beryl. "Think of all that black water," he had said. And she did. Two thousand miles of ocean separated England from New York. "Think how cold it is," he grinned. Beryl hated being cold.

J. C. knew something about Beryl. She was not only fiercely independent but also proud. The fact that others heard his challenge made it more difficult for Beryl to refuse. He offered to pay for the flight, then listed his terms. Beryl must fly solo and nonstop. Otherwise, he wasn't interested. And, he added, she must return his airplane to him in one piece so he could then take off and attempt some flying records of his own.

Beryl remembered how J. C. had grinned at her, "ghoulishly," she said. A solo, nonstop flight across the

Atlantic into dangerous headwinds would require all her strength and mental alertness and courage. That was exactly why it was so tempting. Just as J. C. had anticipated, Beryl accepted his challenge.

At first, it was just an idea, the subject of a conversation among friends. But the idea of flying the Atlantic did not go away. She would need a new airplane for such a long distance flight, a machine that was built to carry additional fuel and maintain altitude with the added weight of the oil and petrol tanks. J. C. had the money to build such a machine. Near the end of 1935, he contracted with Edgar Percival, an airplane manufacturer in England, to begin construction on a Vega Gull cruiser. By February 1936, Beryl was preparing to leave Africa for London.

This was the breakaway point for Beryl, at last. But not just from Blix and elephant safaris. In fact, he would accompany her as a paying passenger on her flight from Nairobi to London. Instead, it was a farewell to Africa. She intended to stay in England, even after her flight. She had saved a little money, thanks to Blix's dangerous assignments. She auctioned off her trusty Avian and got a little more money. Then she visited Elburgon, where her father was managing the Markham stable.

In Beryl's memory, their good-bye was fond, but also frugal. Clutt took her by the arm and led her inside the house where they could talk. He told her that Pegasus had died, possibly from a yellow momba that had entered his stall. She told him about Tom Black winning "the greatest air race ever staged—England to Australia." Clutt's response was that Tom had done "a wonderful thing!"

Yes, but what of Beryl and all she had accomplished? They did not speak of that, nor of the lost days at Njoro or the feelings each had for the other—a father for his free-spirited daughter; a daughter for the father she idolized. It is not clear if she even told Clutt that she was going to London to attempt "a wonderful thing" of her own. About that evening in Elburgon, she wrote: "I rise from my chair and my father glances at the clock. Time for bed. In the morning I will be off, but we have said nothing of good-bye. We have learned frugality—even in this."

The next morning, Beryl climbed into her airplane and took off. She circled, dipping one wing in a salute to her father standing below "shading his eyes, looking upward." He waved once, but not a second time. Beryl leveled off and headed for Nairobi, where Blix was waiting for her.

This good-bye was like no other. For one thing, *arap* Ruta would not be going with her this time. But it was more than that. Africa had changed, and, although she had changed with it, something had been lost. Ten days and six thousand air miles later, Beryl and Blix landed in London. They met Tom and the three raised their glasses in a toast to the land they loved.

You'll see Africa again, Blix assured her.

But those chapters in her life had already been written and were over. "Seeing it again would not be living it again," Beryl wrote. "Africa was gone."

twelve

The Messenger

A new horse with wings was being born. Beryl went often to the factory at Gravesend, England, to watch *The Messenger's* turquoise body and silver wings take shape from wood and metal and fabric. A horserace begins with an animal of good breeding, a thoroughbred born to run. Likewise, Beryl's historic flight across the Atlantic began with the construction of a Vega Gull, designed to fly long distances. Her fuselage, or central body, was longer and wider than standard airplane models. Her undercarriage allowed for additional fuel tanks. She had a total of six tanks, two of which were inside the cabin itself and formed a wall on either side of the cockpit. With that much fuel, a pilot could fly nonstop for 3,800 miles. It was more than enough to make the water-jump from England to the United States, provided the weather cooperated.

Just as a trainer works with a racehorse day after day, judging the animal's strengths and weaknesses and teaching it to respond properly to a jockey's commands, so, too, a pilot and a mechanic work together on a plane, test-flying it for short hops and making mechanical adjustments to ensure a successful flight. *The Messenger* was to have been ready by the end of July so that Beryl could attempt her record-breaking flight in mid-August when the weather would still be favorable. But construction and those minor adjustments had taken longer than anticipated. Beryl's first test flight wasn't until August 15. If she waited much longer, the autumn storms over the North Atlantic could make the waterjump even more dangerous than it already was.

As she watched and waited, she became friendly with the mechanics at Gravesend. Her femininity fooled them at first. At thirty-three, she was six feet tall and willowy thin, with blond wavy hair and cool blue eyes. Her knowledge of flying and of engines impressed them. She did not boast to them about her upcoming flight. In fact, few people beyond her circle of friends that included Tom Black and Jim Mollison knew much about it. It wasn't until Beryl's first test flight in *The Messenger* that the newspapers got wind of the story. Then the reporters descended upon her. Her appearance and her connection to the wealthy Markham family fooled them, also. The headline of an article in the August 18, 1936, edition of the *Daily Express* read: *Society Woman Plans to Fly the Atlantic Alone.*

It was hardly the phrase that Beryl would have chosen to describe herself. Would a society woman have gotten up at dawn to shovel horse manure? Would a society woman have risked her life flying search and rescue missions over the African bush or earned her living by scouting big game by air? Even though the articles mentioned that she had logged more than 2,000 flying hours, the headlines of subsequent articles always emphasized that she was a woman, a mother, or a blond beauty. It angered her. She was a professional pilot. She could navigate. She could strip an engine. Her flight was not a whim nor a publicity stunt. It was a calculated attempt to prove that air transportation across the Atlantic was possible.

Beryl was a private person. She had rarely shared with others the intimate details of her life. Even while living at Mbogani during a separation from Jock Purves, Beryl had not confided in Karen Blixen about her marriage troubles. When Clutt's bankruptcy and the auction of Green Hill Farm had made headlines in Kenya, Beryl had cringed from the publicity. Now, in London, she fled from the cameras. Although Beryl was separated from Mansfield, they were not divorced. Her son Gervase was seven years old, but she had seen him only a few times since his birth. The reporters descended upon the Markhams for their comments, as well. "Gervase is too young to know what his mother is doing," remarked Mansfield discreetly. Indeed, Gervase did not know his mother at all.

Beryl said that she had trained "like an athlete" for her flight. She did not smoke or drink, and she exercised daily to maintain her stamina, for fatigue would be as much a hazard to her as strong headwinds and blinding fog. Tom was married but that did not keep him from becoming Beryl's instructor once again. They spent hours together, studying maps and plotting a route across the ocean. Flying was more than pointing the nose of a plane in one direction and holding her steady. Drift had to be factored into the route. Just as wind creates current and waves in the ocean, so too does wind create currents in the air. Wind direction and speed could push *The Messenger* off course. If visibility were good, Beryl might be able to calculate the amount of drift by watching the movement of the waves on the ocean. If visibility were poor, then Beryl would have to fly blind and trust her instincts and experience to stay on course. "If you misjudge your course only a few degrees," Tom emphasized, "you'll end up in Labrador or in the sea—so don't misjudge anything."

Others assisted in her training, as well. Edgar Percival cautioned her on airlocks. "You know the tanks in the cabin have no gauges, so it may be best to let one run completely dry before opening the next," he told her. "Your motor might go dead in the interval—but she'll start again."

The newspapers did not focus on her training and experience. Instead, one editorial suggested that she give up her plans altogether. Mrs. Markham was risking her life and the worry of an entire nation needlessly, the reporter opined. Those who were with Beryl in those final days before the flight said that she dismissed the article as nonsense and appeared relaxed and fearless. But that was Beryl on the outside. In fact, as August gave way to September and bad weather delayed her flight day after day, Beryl grew anxious and impatient. She was, to use her own word, fidgety. On the evening of September 3, Beryl had dinner with aviator Jim Mollison, airplane manufacturer Edgar Percival, and *The Messenger's* mechanic, Jock Cameron. Tom was out of town, and J. C. Carberry had long ago sailed to New York in order to meet Beryl there when she landed in a blaze of glory at Floyd Bennet Airfield.

At dinner, Beryl told her friends that she could wait no longer. No matter what the weather, she was flying the next day. Percival believed the airplane he had designed could carry her across. Mollison believed in Beryl's flying abilities. He removed his wrist watch, the same watch he had worn while making his attempt across the Atlantic four years earlier. He gave it to her. "For God's sake," Jim said. "Don't get it wet. I want it back!"

Beryl knew what that meant. If the Gull went down over the Atlantic, time would stop completely. No one would ever find her.

The next morning, September 4—a Friday, she was lying in bed in her boarding house room when she received the day's weather forecast. It offered some hope but not much. The west coast of England was still drenched with fog and rain, but a break was anticipated in the afternoon. The break would provide a window through which Beryl could take off. Once airborne, however, she would have to contend with severe thunderstorms over the Atlantic.

For a while, Beryl did not react. She lay in bed, staring at her ceiling and rethinking things. In part, she was flying because of her pride. No one would blame her if she backed down now. The flight was happening too late in the year, and she had had no control over the construction delays or the foul weather. If she bailed out of the agreement now, J. C. might chide her and most definitely the newspapers would write of her change of heart. Those things she could ignore. She thought of Tom and all he had taught her about flying. She would have liked to have spoken with him one more time before deciding if she should go or stay. But Tom was elsewhere. The decision was hers. It had always been hers.

She got out bed, dressed in her gray flannel slacks and a blue silk sport shirt, and over that, pulled on her white aviator suit. Her anxiety in those final few hours before the flight was like the tense moments before a horserace when she had to keep her hands busy to disguise her trembling. But once the gun had sounded and the horses exploded from the gate, Beryl's nervousness had always ceased. Either her horse would win or it would not. That afternoon as she arrived at the Abingdon airfield, Beryl adopted the same attitude. Either she would fly the Atlantic tonight, or she would not. The gun had sounded. She would not turn back.

The mechanics wheeled *The Messenger* out of its hangar. A friend offered her a lifesaving jacket. Beryl considered it. It could keep her afloat for days, but hypothermia from the cold water might kill her all the same. She opted not to take the jacket, but instead to add another layer of warm clothes. The cockpit would be cold, and she hated the cold. Jock Cameron gave her a sprig of heather for good luck. He was her ground mechanic and in the short time that she had known him, she had come to trust him. She wasn't about to refuse his good luck charm. She pinned the heather inside the pocket of her aviator suit.

A few members of the press were there to record her takeoff. *The Messenger* had no radio, and so updates on her progress over the ocean would have to come from ships on the ocean that might spot her plane overhead. Before Beryl snapped on her helmet, she posed for a photograph at the nose of *The Messenger*. One hand was on the two-bladed propeller. Around her neck she had tied a festive polka-dot scarf. But her thin lips were pressed together and her brow was knotted with concentration. She was about to risk her life, and, though danger was exhilarating, she took it seriously.

She handed a sealed envelope to one of the reporters at the airfield. It was a letter she had written explaining her motives and stating clearly that the stereotypes by which the media had labeled her were offensive to her. It is not clear when she wrote the letter—perhaps that very morning after rising from her bed and deciding *Twende tu*—"I'm going" in Swahili. No matter when she had penned it, her statement to the press was emphatic. It must have crossed her mind that these could very well be her final words.

"I have been frequently captioned in the press as 'Society Mother,' 'Flying Mother,' 'Bird Woman,' etc.," she wrote. "The phrase 'society' is repugnant to me. In describing my as yet unaccomplished but no doubt amazing exploit, please give me credit for being an ordinary human being without too many of the conventional virtues. I can laugh, love, and hate. I am neither an innocent girl from the country nor a city slicker, but an ocean flyer in embryo. If I can dispense with the last two words, I will be more than satisfied."

Beryl snapped on her helmet, mounted the airplane's wing, and slipped inside the cockpit. Edgar Percival himself cocked the propeller. Beryl waved good-bye and the horse with wings, weighed down with 1,900 pounds of fuel, taxied down the runway, gained speed, and lifted.

". . . a lone British woman had just taken off from

Abingdon in a single-motored sportplane with an almost suicidal minimum of 260 imperial gallons of gas . . . ," *Time* magazine would later describe the beginning moments of Beryl's flight. In order to carry enough fuel, the article reported, Markham found it necessary to rip out a passenger seat and to go without a radio. "Cocking an eye at the weather report, which indicated increasingly bad storms all the way," the news magazine reported, Markham "soared away into the rain."

The article quoted an American aviator named Harry Richman as remarking gloomily, " 'I don't think she'll get far with a light plane.' "

Thirty minutes into the flight, Beryl knew she was in trouble. The headwinds were driving hard against her, reducing her speed to about ninety miles per hour. At that rate, it would take more than thirty hours to reach North America. *The Messenger* was eating up fuel. After an hour, she crossed the Irish Sea and spied the lights of Cork below. It was night already. A few miles ahead was Berehaven Lighthouse, the last spit of land before the Atlantic. If she were going to abandon her dream and turn back, this was the place. After Berehaven, there would be no solid ground on which to land. But Beryl's doubts and fears from earlier in the day were gone. *The Messenger* bucked and rocked in the wind and pressed on, leaving Ireland behind.

She was flying at 2,000 feet, unable to see beyond the wingtips. Without visibility, she had to fly using her instruments only—an altimeter that recorded the plane's altitude, an artificial horizon that indicated whether the plane was flying level, and of course, her compass. Trust your compass, Tom had taught her, but nothing else. Instruments can go wrong. But don't mistrust the compass—your judgment will never be more accurate than that needle.

It was almost as if he were flying with her.

She tried to climb above the storm, but the rain turned to sleet. Ice coating the wings could cause her to lose control of the airplane. When she dove to a lower altitude, hoping to keep her eye on the movement of the waves and so adjust for drift, the turbulent winds sent her plane into a spin. At one point, Beryl claimed, the wind flipped *The Messenger* and Beryl was flying upside down.

The cockpit cramped her long legs. She barely moved as she worked the pedals, adjusting direction. The cabin was all darkness and roar. When Beryl flew, she often plugged her ears with cotton wool, but that was little help on this journey. She felt as if her ears had gone numb.

After four hours, the engine quit. The first fuel tank was empty. This was expected, though not so soon in the voyage. It was another indication that she was using up too much fuel in flying through the storm. Percival had drilled into her head what she must do next. She slowly pushed the stick forward, lowering the nose. *The Messenger* dove toward the ocean less than 1,500 feet below. Losing altitude was necessary in order to maintain enough speed and avoid stalling. She must turn off the petcock, or valve, on the empty tank before opening another. She kept her eyes on the altimeter as her fingers fumbled in the dark near the floor of the cabin for the pin. At one thousand feet, she found the petcock and turned.

Nothing happened.

"She'll start again," Percival had assured her, but at 500 feet, with lightning flashing around her, *The Messenger* was still diving. At 300 feet, the engine suddenly kicked into life again. Beryl pulled back on the stick and began her climb.

Five fuel tanks remained. It was going to be a long, lonely night.

She had packed some cold chicken in a cardboard box, but the strong winds made it impossible to concentrate on anything but maintaining control of the airplane. The small box of food was just far enough away to make reaching for it dangerous. The storm was hours behind her now but still the fog blinded her. The coffee helped some. But at dawn an air pocket caused her to spill what was left of it. Beryl felt as if she were about to cry. She couldn't do it any longer. She had been flying blind for more than nineteen hours. The roar of the engine vibrated inside her head. Fatigue and "the waste of sky and water" had finally defeated her. She could not turn back, but she could not continue, either.

Still the engine roared.

Beryl's head felt heavy. Her eyes burned as if gritty with the red dust of Njoro. During the long night, she thought of Africa and her father, Kibii and *arap* Maina, Buller and her horses—all the things that had happened to her and had carried her to this moment. But mostly she thought about the weather and wished it would clear up, wished the fog would break so she could see. She could not go on. She was cold, desperately cold. Her thermos of coffee had spilled. It was Beryl's worst moment.

In her pocket, Jim Mollison's watch—still dry—ticked. Beryl forced back her tears. The wind was shifting. Below her, the fog was breaking up, and she spied a ship on the ocean below. It was the first sign of life she had seen since passing over Berehaven Lighthouse. The ship was a freighter. The captain had spied her airplane as well— though Beryl had no way of knowing that—and radioed her location. The Radio Corporation of America intercepted his message: "Airplane, probably Mrs. Markham's, passed the *S.S. Spaarndam* at 7 A.M., E.S.T., position 47:54 N., 48:22 W., heading for Newfoundland."

Beryl was 1,500 miles from New York. The wind-battered *Messenger* was still flying high and on course, though, of course, Beryl had no way of knowing that, either.

The sunlight and the ship renewed her spirits. "I stopped being so silly," Beryl said. She was going to make it, after all. "' . . . If you stay awake,'" she told herself, "'you'll find it's only a matter of time now.'" She made another entry in her logbook, then began to plot a new course for clearly she would need to land to refuel. By her new estimation, she had used twenty-seven hours of fuel in less than twenty-four hours. She studied her map. Sydney was the closest airfield. She decided to land there. Although she was chilled to the bone and weary, she would not stop to rest. After refueling, she'd push on to New York and Floyd Bennet Field where J. C. was waiting.

She began to hum. The worst part of the voyage was behind her at last.

Suddenly, like Wise Child, so close to victory all at once faltering on the track, the Vega Gull engine shuddered and stumbled in the sky. Somehow Wise Child had recovered and limped on. *The Messenger* tried. The engine caught and the plane climbed. But then *The Messenger* sputtered again and began to fall again.

"There are words for everything," Beryl said. "There was a word for this—airlock." She twisted the petcocks of each tank off and on, hoping to clear whatever it was that had clogged the fuel line and was causing the engine to choke. But she was losing altitude. She reached for the flask of brandy and took two good swallows.

Through the ribbons of fog she saw cliffs reaching up for her. Land was dead ahead, perhaps less than fifty miles. If she could only make it that far, her life, at least, would be saved. And yet, even as she worked to engage the engine still again, bitter disappointment filled her. After pushing so hard and coming so far, she was going to lose. Her goal had been New York. "There are words for everything," Beryl had said, and the word for a forced landing short of a pilot's destination is failure.

The engine caught, and Beryl breathed again as the plane climbed a few hundred feet. Then once more, the Vega Gull quit.

"This time she's dead as death; the Gull settles earthward and it isn't any earth I know," Beryl wrote. "It is black earth stuck with boulders and I hang above it, on hope and on a motionless propeller."

She cleared the rocks, then banked. She saw what

appeared from the air to be an open green field. *The Messenger* glided low, and Beryl set her down. Too late, she realized she had been deceived. The green field was, in fact, a mossy bog. The plane ploughed into the muck and drove for forty feet. Then the left wheel sank, throwing *The Messenger* into a nosedive. Thrust forward, Beryl cracked her forehead against the glass and lost consciousness.

thirteen

The Stranger

A gash on her forehead between her eyes was bleeding badly. Blood covered her face and stained the front of her aviator's suit. Beryl struggled out of the cockpit, then crawled down the side of the airplane's wing. She sank up to her knees in mud. She had crashed in "a nameless swamp," but it was land, at least. She gazed first at her watch and counted the hours she had flown nonstop: twenty-one and twenty-five minutes. Then she looked at *The Messenger.* The force of the crash had driven the plane's nose into the bog so that the fuselage and tail stuck at an angle in the air. The landing gear was gone; the propeller seemed bent. Beryl's horse with wings was crippled. It could not fly again. Dazed, Beryl struggled through the marsh in search of help.

A fisherman found her. She was on Cape Breton, Nova Scotia, he told her. And she told him how she had gotten there. She had just flown the Atlantic in twenty-one hours and twenty-five minutes, nonstop.

She needed a telephone, she said. People were waiting to hear from her. She had to get to New York where they were expecting her. The fisherman took her to a farm-house. The local doctor who examined Beryl said she was suffering from exhaustion and quite possibly a concussion. He stitched and bandaged the laceration on her forehead, then ordered her to stay in bed for twenty-four hours. Beryl had no clothes except what she had worn under her aviator's suit. Someone loaned her a pair of pajamas and served her a cup of tea.

She hadn't slept for forty hours. She could not sleep now. A little more than four hours was the best she could do. One thought kept gnawing at her. She had failed. She had failed to reach New York, and she had failed to return J. C.'s plane in one piece. *The Messenger* was still stranded in the bog. Leave it, J. C. had told her when she finally reached him in New York by telephone. Forget it, he said.

But that was the problem. She couldn't forget it. She couldn't stop thinking of how it had all gone wrong in the last stretch. She couldn't stop wishing that it had not ended this way.

What Beryl felt was a personal failure, however, the world viewed as an amazing accomplishment. The word of her successful waterjump was radioed to England and Europe, even as far as Africa. By the next morning, dozens of cablegrams of congratulations began to arrive from all over the world. Newspapers on both sides of the ocean covered the story and quoted from the letter Beryl had given to the reporter in Abington before taking off. FLIGHT ASTONISHES THE BRITISH PUBLIC read one headline. Also published in the newspapers were statements from people who knew Beryl. A reporter quoted that Mansfield Markham was overjoyed at his wife's success. "The flight is a magnificent achievement," he said, "although it must have been a great disappointment to her to have failed to reach New York."

"Amazing!" was Tom Black's enthusiastic exclamation.

The London *Daily Express* had even reached Beryl's father in faraway Africa. "This is the happiest day of my life," the newspaper quoted Clutt. "I knew she would triumph, but in spite of my faith in her abilities, yesterday was the most anxious day I have known."

What must Beryl have thought when she read her father's words? That he had faith in her abilities would not have surprised her. On Green Hill Farm, he had always expected much from her and she had not disappointed him. That he had been anxious for her safety during the flight would not have surprised her either. Her father cared for her. No, what must have touched Beryl, deeply, was that the happiest day of her father's life had been her triumph in flying the Atlantic.

Two days before at the Abington airfield in England, only a few curious spectators and a handful of newspaper reporters had gathered to see her off. Now thousands of fans crowded the airfield in Halifax, Nova Scotia, to get a glimpse of her as she prepared to board a plane for New York. She was dressed once again in her gray slacks and blue shirt open at the neck and with the sleeves rolled above her elbows. She wore a watch on each wrist.

Beryl preferred privacy to publicity, and the surging crowds surprised her. She was still brooding over her own failure, and the clamor for her autograph left her uneasy. The scene was repeated at a number of stops along the way. By the time Beryl arrived at Floyd Bennet Field in

New York that Sunday afternoon, 150 policemen had formed a protective line to hold back the crowd of five thousand people. It was not J. C.'s *The Messenger* that had brought her to them. But they did not care. That she had flown the Atlantic and made the continent was good enough. In fact, it was spectacular. She was the first person—man or woman—to have flown from England to Canada, east to west across the Atlantic, and the throng of well-wishers roared with delight at seeing her.

"Hello, Blondie!" the crowd shouted.

A little stunned by the adoration, Beryl gave in to their cheers. She lifted both her arms and bowed to them in a traditional African *salaam*. All the while, the cameras clicked.

In the golden age of flying, Beryl Markham had become a hero.

J. C. and his wife, Maia, were at the airfield. Beryl and Maia embraced, then the police ushered them quickly to the waiting automobiles. J. C. had booked a suite for Beryl at the Ritz-Carlton Hotel in New York City. Outside the hotel, more curious spectators waited. As Beryl stepped from the automobile, the crowd applauded her. "How about a drink of orange juice?" someone called to her.

Beryl laughed. "Oh, I think I'd like something a little stronger," she answered. "I'd like a champagne cocktail."

"The tall and sprightly blonde bounded into the hotel lobby," *The New York Times* reported, where the hotel management immediately served her the champagne she had requested. Beryl drank it "with gusto."

But once in the privacy of her hotel room, away from the crowds and the cameras, Beryl sank to the sofa. She was not smiling now. Her head ached, and she shook it. "Never again," she said. Those who were with her caught the grave tone of her voice and saw the nervous strain of the last forty-eight hours on her face. For a few moments, Beryl had let down her guard.

The doctor arrived and examined her. He changed the bandage on her forehead and on her hands where the petcocks' pins had scratched her. She was suffering from nervous exhaustion, he said. She must rest.

In the morning, Beryl was interviewed for the newsreels. In 1936, before television, newsreels were shown in movie theaters across the country before the main feature. But she was nervous in front of the movie camera and at times seemed puzzled as to what to say in answer to the reporters' questions. The taping had to be redone three times. Clearly, Beryl was still fatigued though she complained, "I'm tired of all this resting business."

"What did you think of up there over the ocean?" a reporter asked.

"Lots of unpleasant things," she answered. "The weather," she said. "I kept wishing it would get warmer, because it got desperately cold out there some time before I got to Nova Scotia and these were all the clothes I had."

In answer to another question, she said she had had nothing to eat, just a swig of brandy.

"Just one swig?" the reporter asked.

Beryl laughed. "Two, I'm afraid."

"Are you planning a future as an aviator for your son?"

If the question surprised her in its assumption that

Beryl was a warm and caring mother to Gervase, she didn't reveal any awkwardness in her reply. "Surely," she nodded. "By the time he's grown, I expect we'll all be crossing the Atlantic by air, and certainly by that time we will have regular mail service."

She had turned the question to her favorite point of argument in discussing why she had flown the Atlantic. Her father had been a pioneer of East Africa. She was a pioneer, too, of the skies.

Each day, the newspapers reported on Mrs. Markham's activities in New York City. She was the guest of honor at luncheons and dinner dances. To attend one dinner in her honor, the newspaper reported, she had borrowed an evening gown.

A few days later, the mayor of New York City, Fiorello La Guardia, honored Beryl in a special ceremony held on the steps outside City Hall. Once again, a reporter's movie camera captured the moment. The black and white newsreel shows Beryl descending the steps to a bank of microphones. Her appearance is much changed. Gone are the sporty slacks and the shirt with its rolled-up sleeves. Instead, she is wearing a print suit and a blouse that has a bow tie and ruffles down the front. Under her left arm, pressed against her body, is her clutch purse. She looks less like an aviator and more like the society woman that the British newspapers had accused her of being. But her forehead is still bandaged. In front of the microphones, she stands a foot taller than the mayor.

"Mrs. Markham," he begins, "may I on behalf of the city of New York extend to you a sincere welcome and our congratulations on your splendid flight across the ocean."

He shakes her hand and the cameras flash and keep flashing.

Beryl's response is clipped. "Thank you so much. I'm so happy to be here."

She had run out of things to say.

The reporters continued to photograph her and the mayor. "Shake hands again," they said, and again the cameras clicked. Finally, Beryl had turned to them and said dryly, "Do you mind?"

Enough was enough.

Although she attended parties and gave interviews and rode in a ticker-tape parade held in her honor, she couldn't stop wishing that she had not run out of petrol. In her world of absolutes, to have almost made it to Floyd Bennet Field just wasn't good enough.

"It was just beastly weather," she tried to explain. "Wind and rain and fog, hour after hour."

The thing that overcame Beryl's disappointment in herself, that made her sense of failure seem insignificant after all, was the shocking news she received only a few days after her flight across the Atlantic. Jim Mollison called her from England with the terrible news. Tom Black had been killed in his airplane in England. He died not in the air, but on the ground as he taxied into position for take-off. Another airplane that was landing simply did not see him, nor did Tom see it. The blade of the on-coming plane sliced through the cockpit and into Tom's heart.

Although he had not been at Abington to see her off, he had been with her in spirit during the long night and day over the Atlantic. "The knowledge of my hands on the controls," Beryl wrote, had been Tom's knowledge.

The Stranger

That Tom was dead did not seem possible.

It was time to go home, Beryl realized, though she wasn't sure anymore where home was. Her father and Ada had left Kenya once again and were living now in South Africa. Mansfield Markham and her son were in England, but that was a door Beryl had closed and did not wish to open again. Nor was Mansfield eager for a reconciliation. Still another article in *The New York Times* had been printed with this headline: MARKHAM REUNION DOUBTED. It was a small piece, tucked under another longer story about Beryl. It read:

According to the Daily Express, Mrs. Beryl Markham's broken romance will not be mended by the triumph of her flight. . . . Although Mansfield Markham, the wealthy young film producer who wooed and won her in Kenya nine years ago, but from whom she is now separated, talked with her over the Atlantic telephone, there is said to be no possibility of a reunion. Mr. Markham and his seven-year-old son, Gervase, have gone away to escape the crowds.

Beryl's romance with Mansfield had long ago ended. The newspaper said nothing about the respect and the love she still had for Tom Campbell Black. Beryl had left Africa and *arap* Ruta to live in England and to attempt a grand thing—flying over the ocean east to west. But she had also come to England to be near Tom. His death was not the first painful loss Beryl had experienced. Even without Tom, life would go on. It always did.

What will you do now? the reporters, who still followed her, asked. By now, they had uncovered a bit of her past—her reputation in Kenya as a horse trainer; her years as a commercial pilot. What will be your next adventure?

She wasn't sure. She had lost *The Messenger* in six feet of mud on Cape Breton. Souvenir hunters had stripped the fabric from its wings and removed most of the movable parts and the Royal Mounted Canadian Police were now guarding it. Beryl did not have the money to purchase the Vega Gull from J. C. and salvage it. She might visit her father, she thought. Some people in Hollywood had suggested that she work for them as an adviser for flying films. Or perhaps she could even star in a film of her own, "portraying her great achievement" as an aviator. Someone else proposed that Beryl write a book about her extraordinary life.

Write a book . . . now that interested her. But to write her memoir meant taking a close look at herself, where she had been and how she had come to be the person she was. Beryl was a risk-taker, a free-spirit. But she was something else, too: a stranger to herself.

"You can live a lifetime and, at the end of it, know more about other people than you know about yourself," Beryl said. "You learn to watch other people, but you never watch yourself because you strive against loneliness. . . ."

Beryl's free-spirited behavior was more complicated than just wanting to feel alive, though that was part of it. As *Lakweit*, she had run and hunted with *arap* Maina, because in running and hunting she could escape the lonely life with no mother and a father who had other worries on his mind besides his daughter. As *Memsahib wa Farasi*, she had worked from sunrise to sunset training her racehorses, because in working hard she did not have the time to be alone with herself. She tested her own endurance at the controls of an airplane for the same reason. But eventually, loneliness caught up with her.

"Being alone in an aeroplane for even so short a time as a night and day, irrevocably alone, with nothing to observe but your instruments and your own hands in semi-darkness, nothing to contemplate but the size of your small courage, nothing to wonder about but the beliefs, the faces, and the hopes rooted in your mind—such an experience can be as startling as the first awareness of a stranger walking by your side at night. You are the stranger."

Perhaps one day she would write about her life. She had kept her logbooks and cablegrams and newspaper clips. She had her memories of East Africa. But she was not ready to write her memoir just now. She needed a little more time to figure things out, to decide which memories were worth putting into print and which were best tucked away and left unspoken.

Less than a week after Tom's death, Beryl boarded the *Queen Mary,* an ocean liner bound for England. She was given a first-class cabin. While in New York City, she had acquired a wardrobe of fashionable clothes, no doubt from well-wishers and admirers, including J. C. and Maia. A photograph taken one evening during dinner at the captain's table shows Beryl dressed in a white satin gown with puff sleeves. Despite the dress-up clothes, the elegant dinners, and the ballroom dancing, this long, slow crossing of the ocean must have been just as unnerving for Beryl as flying alone in an airplane for one night and day had been. Perhaps it was more lonely, for her great achievement was now behind her and what lay ahead was uncertain, except for one thing. Tom would not be in London to meet her when she arrived.

Once not so long ago, she and Tom and Blix had sat together in a restaurant in London and raised their glasses in a toast to Africa, because Africa was gone. What was left for her now? Upon whom could she depend now? There was only one thing, one person: herself.

Her life had always been that way. Depending on yourself was the lesson *arap* Maina had taught her so long ago in the African bush. It was what she learned also from her father as she watched him tie the goat to a thorn tree to bait the leopards that had killed his greyhounds. Beryl had never been the goat in life. Although at times she had been afraid and unsure, she had never cowered.

When the *Queen Mary* docked in England in late September 1936, reporters were waiting for Beryl. But their numbers were not as large as in New York. Already her candle of fame was burning down. But Beryl accepted that, too. That was the wisdom of the egret's message given to her by her one true friend, Kibii. All her tomorrows could not be like all her yesterdays. Well, she would just have to go on inventing her tomorrows.

As Beryl faced the cameras and the reporters, she slipped on her skin of confidence and she smiled.

Epilogue

In 1939, after trying unsuccessfully to locate *arap* Ruta in Kenya, Beryl booked passage on a ship and returned to the United States. She accepted a job as an advisor for a film called *Safari*, set in Africa and starring one of Hollywood's leading men—Douglas Fairbanks Jr. In Hollywood, Beryl lived a glamorous life and a rather lazy one in comparison to the daring adventures of her past. Her position as advisor on the film was more fun than work. She dined with actors and actresses, and partied on the beaches with scriptwriters and poets. In 1941, she met a writer named Raoul Schumacher. With his assistance, Beryl wrote her memoir, *West with the Night*. In her book, Beryl fondly described the Africa of her childhood, the Africa that she had lost. Not surprisingly, she dedicated the book to her father. Published in 1942, *West with the Night* received immediate critical acclaim. American writer Ernest Hemingway called it "a bloody wonderful book." Soon after the book's publication, Mansfield Markham divorced Beryl. The day after her divorce, Beryl married Raoul.

Like most of the shooting stars in Beryl's life, the fame sparked by her book soon faded. The attraction between

Beryl and Raoul also began to fade. Although they often worked together—Beryl dictating stories of growing up in British East Africa while Raoul copied them down—Beryl complained that he drank too much. They argued. Eventually, her third marriage ended as the others had, in divorce.

In 1952, Beryl returned at last to the place that was home after all, Kenya. Once more, she was facing an uncertain future. Once more, she was in need of money. And once more, she called upon the hospitality of old friends who gave her a place to live until she could figure out what to do next. She tried odd jobs, including working a short time as a secretary. She tried writing and selling a few short stories in order to earn some money, but magazine publishers rejected her work. What Beryl knew and loved best was not writing. It was horses. She hunted down *arap* Ruta and persuaded her father, who was then living in South Africa, and perhaps even her former husband, Mansfield Markham, to invest in her new stable of horses.

A few years later, her father died. He left everything he owned to his wife, Ada. Everything, that is, except his best horse. And that he willed to Beryl.

Beryl's life had a rhythm to it, a refrain marked by loss, rebellion, and then achievement that repeated itself over and over. By 1958 and throughout the 1960s, with Ruta by her side, the thoroughbreds in Mrs. Markham's stables were once again in the winner's circle. The 1963-64 racing season was one of her best, with forty-six winning horses. But the cycle was about to repeat itself. She gave all her attention to her horses and little to her finances. Beryl seemed to share the same attitude toward money as the Africans who had stood in line on pay day at Green Hill Farm. The few coins Clutt counted out into their palms were either paid in taxes to the British government or buried in the ground as worthless trinkets. Beryl always spent whatever money she earned.

By 1980, she was once again living in squalor with only a few horses in her stables. But Beryl's strength was that she dared to achieve again. "A life has to move or it stagnates," she once said. Beryl had never allowed her life to stagnate. In 1983, the republication of her book *West with the Night* brought her new wealth and worldwide fame.

In her 80s, the woman who was once *Lakweit* continued to rise at dawn in the African highlands, to breathe deeply the sharp, cold air, and to train horses. Beryl Markham died in Kenya on August 3, 1986, at the age of 83.

Acknowledgments

For valuable feedback on this book, I wish to thank my former executive editor at Weekly Reader Corporation, Nancy Webb. I also wish to thank my colleagues Kathleen White and Kate Davis who read and listened as I found the right threads to weave Beryl's story. In researching details of Beryl's life not covered in *West with the Night*, I owe my gratitude to the thorough books written by Beryl's biographers: Mary Lovell, *Straight on Till Morning*, and Errol Trzebinski, *The Lives of Beryl Markham*. Finally, I wish to thank Farrar, Straus, and Giroux for permission to quote the copyrighted material by Beryl Markham from *West with the Night*.

Chronology of Beryl Markham's Life

1902   Beryl Clutterbuck born in England.

1904   Beryl's father, Charles Clutterbuck, emigrates to British East Africa.

1906   Beryl's mother, Clara Clutterbuck, leaves British East Africa and returns to England.

1909   Ada Orchardson comes to live at the Clutterbuck farm in Njoro.

1914   The Great War begins.

1919   Beryl marries Jock Purvis.

1920   The bankrupted Clutterbuck farm is auctioned and Beryl's father and Ada leave BEA for South America.

1926   Beryl, separated from her husband, wins the St. Leger horserace in Nairobi.

1927   Beryl marries Mansfield Markham.

1929   Beryl gives birth to a son, Gervase Markham, in England.

1931   Denys Finch Hatton dies in a plane crash; Beryl flies an airplane solo for the first time.

1933   Beryl earns her B license under British regulations and becomes a commercial pilot.

1936   Beryl leaves Africa for England and accepts dare to fly solo west across the Atlantic.

1939   Beryl returns to the United States to become an advisor for *Safari,* a Hollywood movie set in Africa.

1942   Beryl divorces Mansfield Markham, marries her third husband, and publishes *West with The Night,* a memoir of her life in British East Africa.

1952   Divorced from her third husband, Beryl returns alone to British East Africa—now called Kenya.

1964   Kenya becomes a republic and elects as its first president, Jomo Kenyatta, a Kikuyu leader.

1960s   Beryl Markham continues to train and race horses in Nairobi.

1986   Beryl Markham dies in her home.

Selected Sources

Adamson, Joy. *The Peoples of Kenya*. New York: Harcourt, Brace & World, Inc. 1967.

"Aerodynamic Diana," *Time,* July 20, 1942.

Beard, Peter H. *The End of the Game: The Last Word from Paradise*. New York: Doubleday, 1977.

Buchanan, Lamont. *The Flying Years*. New York: Putnam's Sons, 1953.

Curle, Capt. A. T. "When a Drought Blights Africa," *National Geographic*. April, 1929.

Isak Dinesen. *Out of Africa*. New York: Random House. 1965.

Isak Dinesen's Africa: Images of the Wild Continent from the Writer's Life and Words. San Francisco: Sierra Club Books. 1985.

Hahn, Emily. "My Dear Selous . . ." *American Heritage,* April, 1963.

Huxley, Elspeth. *The Flames Trees of Thika: Memories of an African Childhood*. New York: William Morrow and Company, 1959.

Huxley, Elspeth. *Nellie: Letters from Africa*. London: Weidenfeld and Nicolson. 1973.

Huxley, Elspeth. *Nine Faces of Kenya: Portrait of a Nation*. New York: Viking, 1990.

Lovell, Mary S. *Straight on Till Morning: The Biography of Beryl Markham*. New York: St. Martin's Press. 1987.

Maren, Michael. *The Land and People of Kenya.* New York: J. B. Lippincott. 1989.

Markham, Beryl. "Something I Remember," *Collier's,* January 29, 1944.

Markham, Beryl. "The Splendid Outcast," *The Saturday Evening Post,* Jan/Feb 1990.

Markham, Beryl. *West with the Night.* New York: North Point Press. 1983.

Miller, Charles. *The Lunatic Express.* New York: Macmillan. 1971.

New York Times, articles from September 6, 7, and 8, 1936.

Smith, Anthony. *The Great Rift: Africa's Changing Valley.* New York: Sterling Pub. Co. 1988.

Stott, Kenhelm W., Jr. *Exploring with Martin and Osa Johnson.* Chaute, Kansas: Martin and Osa Johnson Safari Museum Press, 1978.

"Transatlantic Types," *Time* 28:11, September 14, 1936.

Trzebinski, Errol. *The Lives of Beryl Markham.* New York: W.W. Norton & Co., 1993.

Turnbull, Colin M. *Tradition and Change in African Tribal Life.* New York: The World Publishing Company, 1966.

Queeny, Edgar Monsanto. "Spearing Lions with Africa's Masai," *The National Geographic Magazine* Vol: CVI, 4, October, 1954.

World Without Walls: Beryl Markham's African Memoir. SHG Productions. 1985.

Index

THE BARNARD BIOGRAPHY SERIES

The Barnard Biography Series expands the universe of heroic women with these profiles. The details of each woman's life may vary, but each was led by a bold spirit and an active intellect to engage her particular world. All have left inspiring legacies that are captured in these biographies.

Barnard College is a selective, independent liberal arts college for women affiliated with Columbia University and located in New York City. Founded in 1889, it was among the pioneers in the crusade to make higher education available to young women. Over the years, its alumnae have become leaders in the fields of public affairs, the arts, literature, and science. Barnard's enduring mission is to provide an environment conducive to inquiry, learning, and expression while also fostering women's abilities, interests, and concerns.

Other titles in *The Barnard Biography Series:*

Elizabeth Blackwell: A Doctor's Triumph